30-SECOND
BIBLE

30-SECOND
BIBLE

The 50 most meaningful moments
in the Bible, each explained in
half a minute

Editor
Russell Re Manning

Contributors
Stefan Bosman
Liz Gulliford
Tim Muldoon
Russell Re Manning
Andrew D. Swafford

METRO BOOKS
NEW YORK

METRO BOOKS
New York

An Imprint of Sterling Publishing
387 Park Avenue South
New York, NY 10016

This book was conceived,
designed, and produced by

Ivy Press
210 High Street, Lewes,
East Sussex BN7 2NS, U.K.
www.ivypress.co.uk

Creative Director **Peter Bridgewater**
Publisher **Jason Hook**
Editorial Director **Caroline Earle**
Art Director **Michael Whitehead**
Designer **Ginny Zeal**
Illustrator **Ivan Hissey**
Profiles Text **Russell Re Manning**
Glossaries Text **Nick Fawcett**
Project Editor **Jamie Pumfrey**

ISBN: 978-1-4351-4346-3

CONTENTS

INTRODUCTION
Russell Re Manning

The best-selling book of all time, no single work
has had more impact on world culture than the Bible. It is ubiquitous and
familiar, with its stories retold in some of the greatest artwork in history,
its law-codes influencing legal systems around the world, and its verses
informing the languages we speak—not to mention its pivotal role in
Judaism and Christianity. And yet, the Bible is also something of a mystery
to many people, full of half-remembered stories, strange characters,
and endless off-putting lists of so-and-so begetting so-and-so.
Misconceptions abound about when the Bible was written, by whom,
and for what purpose. Controversies are rife over how to translate and
interpret the Bible, and there is not even consensus among Christians
about which books are in and which are out. In a sense, this is hardly
surprising for a work written and compiled over many centuries and held
by two of the world's great religions to be divinely inspired, but it certainly
can be confusing. Fortunately, this book can help.

How the book works

In the pages that follow, fifty key biblical passages are explained in plain
English, without jargon or religious bias. In each case, the story and
significance is set out accessibly and engagingly in less time than it takes
to spell Nebuchadnezzar. Each 30-second explanation is presented
alongside a 3-second sermon summing up the take-home message in
a single sentence, and a 3-minute meditation for those with more time
to reflect upon the meaning of the "Good Book." There is also a key
quotation from the relevant passage and references to related stories.

The entries are organized into seven chapters. We begin **In the
Beginning,** with the opening narratives of the Bible, from Creation itself
through Adam and Eve and the stories of the earliest biblical characters
up to Noah and his sons. In **The Promised Land,** we trace the story of
God's covenant with His chosen people, from Abram (Abraham) to Moses.
Biblical History tells the history of the ancient kingdoms of Israel and

Old and new

*The Bible is divided into
two main sections: the Old
Testament is concerned
mainly with the Law and
Prophets, the New with
the ministry of Jesus and
life of the early Church.
This book will help you
find your way around the
Old and New Testament,
and what's in between.*

THE BOOKS OF THE OLD TESTAMENT[1]

The Pentateuch
Genesis
Exodus
Leviticus
Numbers
Deuteronomy

The Historical Books
Joshua
Judges
Ruth
1 Samuel
2 Samuel
1 Kings
2 Kings
1 Chronicles
2 Chronicles
Ezra
Nehemiah
Esther

The Poetical and Wisdom Books
Job
Psalms
Proverbs
Ecclesiastes
Song of Solomon

The Prophetic Books
Isaiah
Jeremiah
Lamentations
Ezekiel
Daniel
Hosea
Joel
Amos
Obadiah
Jonah
Micah
Nahum
Habakkuk
Zephaniah
Haggai
Zechariah
Malachi

THE BOOKS OF THE NEW TESTAMENT[1]

The Gospels
Matthew
Mark
Luke
John

The Acts of the Apostles

The Epistles[2]
Romans
1 Corinthians
2 Corinthians
Galatians
Ephesians
Philippians
Colossians -
1 Thessalonians

2 Thessalonians
1 Timothy
2 Timothy
Titus
Philemon
Hebrews
James
1 Peter
2 Peter
1 John
2 John
3 John
Jude

Revelation

1 Listed according to the New Revised Standard Version
2 Romans to Philemon are all attributed to Paul; Hebrews is anonymous.

Judah and of the prophets with their repeated calls for ethical and religious righteousness. In **Words of Wisdom**, we turn to some of the most poetic and philosophical writings in the Old Testament, from the Psalms, Proverbs, and Song of Solomon to the haunting story of the trials of Job. The final three chapters deal with the New Testament. In **A New Testament**, the key moments in Jesus' life are covered, from the Annunciation and nativity to the Last Supper, trial, and the Crucifixion. **The Son of God** takes us through a selection of Jesus' parables and miracles. The final chapter, **The Birth of Christianity**, explores the beginnings of Christianity as a religion and moves from the Gospels to the book of Acts, the Epistles, and the last book of the Bible, the apocalyptic book of Revelation. Along the way, we meet seven key biblical figures, including Satan and St. Paul. Seven chapters, then, that take us from the beginning to the end of the world in under half an hour.

Just as the Bible can be read in many different ways, so, too, can this book. If you read it cover to cover, you'll get an overview of the amazing range and diversity of the Bible, and of some of the often-surprising interconnections between passages. Read more selectively, it will help you to explore individual stories and characters. Sometimes this will be like a walk down memory lane, rediscovering half-remembered nuggets from Sunday school; other stories will be new discoveries or provide fresh details finally filling a gap in your knowledge—for example, why Jonah was eaten by a whale (or was it really a whale?) and where the idea of "speaking in tongues" comes from.

What is the Bible?

But before we take up the Bible and read, we need to step back and return to the most basic question: What is the Bible? The most useful approach is to define it as the collection of primary texts of Judaism and Christianity. There is no single agreed common version—accepted Christian Bibles range from sixty-six to eighty-one books. That said, all Christian Bibles are divided into Old and New Testaments, with some including the Apocrypha, or "intertestamental" writings, between the two. For Jews, only thirty books of the Christian Old Testament are canonical (that is, accepted as Scripture).

The Tanakh—as the Old Testament is called in Hebrew—is divided into three parts: the Torah (meaning "Teaching"), the Nevi'im (meaning "Prophets"), and Ketuvim (meaning "Writings"). The Torah comprises the

Sacred texts

In Jewish synagogues even today, the so-called Torah—most sacred of the Hebrew Scriptures containing the first five books of the Old Testament—is typically hand-written on parchment scrolls, stored in a cabinet called the Holy Ark.

first five books of the Old Testament, from Genesis to Deuteronomy, known as the Pentateuch and traditionally held to have been written by Moses. These books contain the dramatic accounts of the prehistory of the Jews up to the covenant of God with His chosen people, and details of the Law, as given to Moses on Mount Sinai. The Nevi'im tells the history of the Jewish monarchy up until the exile in Babylon and the destruction of the Temple, interspersing battles and politics with constant reminders from the prophets of God's will. The books that make up the Ketuvim include poetic and philosophical writings, probably composed during or after the Babylonian exile. A rich mixture of genres and styles, the writings of the Tanakh combine ancient mythology with legal codes, national history, poetry, prophesy, and theology, all united by the common thread of Jewish ethical monotheism.

Written in Hebrew (with some short portions in Aramaic), the Tanakh was given a prominent place in Christianity from the outset and is quoted in the New Testament in the third-century-BCE Greek translation known as the Septuagint (the name is derived from the seventy scholars said to have produced it). The New Testament, written in Greek between 50 and 150 CE, is no more homogeneous than the Old. Containing twenty-seven books, it is divided into the four Gospels, the book of Acts, twenty-one Epistles, and the book of Revelation.

The Gospels

The Gospels (from the Old English *god-spell*, meaning "good news," itself a translation of the Greek *euangelion—eu-* "good" and *-angelion* "message"), are a unique genre; both historical biography and theological commentary, they recount the life, teaching, and miracles of Jesus, from the announcement of his birth to his Resurrection appearances, and were probably written for particular communities of Christians associated with different apostles in the years following Jesus' death. The New Testament contains four canonical Gospels—Matthew, Mark, Luke, and John—but there are many similar texts, known as the "apocryphal Gospels." The idea of four canonical Gospels was first championed by the second-century theologian Irenaeus of Lyons, and confirmed in the fifth century. Strikingly, there are many parallels between the four canonical Gospels, including word-for-word overlaps. The similarities are greatest between Matthew, Mark, and Luke, which are referred to as the "Synoptic Gospels," indicating that they can be read together. Mark is

New Testament texts
An ancient papyrus put up for sale by an Egyptian trader in Cairo in 1930 contains text written in Greek from many or Paul's letters, including 2 Corinthians 11.33–12.9 shown here.

Illuminated manuscripts
An image of Christ enthroned from the Book of Kells, *a spectacular illuminated (illustrated) manuscript of the Gospels that was created by Celtic monks in ca.800. Such beautiful books were treasured possessions, made of vellum (prepared animal skins) by teams of specialist scribes and illustrators, and are among the masterpieces of medieval art.*

thought to be the earliest and overlaps extensively with Matthew and Luke. Some scholars have speculated about a further text, now lost, that was a common source for these two (they term it Q, an abbreviation of the German *Quelle*, meaning "source"), but its existence is hotly disputed. John's Gospel, also known as "the Fourth Gospel," stands apart from the others, having a distinctive theological approach, encapsulated by its poetic "prologue": "In the beginning was the Word, and the Word was with God, and the Word was God" (John 1.1).

The book of Acts, also known as the Acts of the Apostles, tells the story of the early Christians. Probably written by the same author who wrote Luke's Gospel, Acts recounts the missionary activity of the twelve apostles and of Paul of Tarsus, whose conversion experience is also included. Paul dominates the Epistles (from the Greek meaning "letter"), which comprise the bulk of the New Testament books. Written to newly established Christian communities around the Mediterranean, these letters contain a mixture of practical and pastoral advice, and they have been fundamental for the development of Christian theology. The final book of the New Testament is Revelation (not Revelations), an apocalyptic vision of the end of the world (it takes its title from its first word, *apokalypsis*, meaning "unveiling" or "revelation"). This dramatic work, full of elaborate symbolism and intricate predictions, is described as written on the island of Patmos by "John," who is traditionally identified with the author of John's Gospel.

Translating the Scriptures

Since their composition, the books of the Bible have been translated into virtually every language of the world, but three translations have had a particular significance. The fourth-century-CE translation into Latin by St. Jerome, known as the Vulgate, is the official Bible of the Roman Catholic Church, and for centuries before the Reformation, it was the only widely available form of the Bible in Western Europe. That changed, however, with Luther's German translation. While Luther was not the first to translate the Bible into the vernacular, his was the most important such translation, and subsequent Protestant Bibles followed his lead in excluding the intertestamental Apocrypha. In the English-speaking world, the greatest impact was made by the so-called King James or Authorized Version (AV), produced between 1604 and 1611 by a team of forty-seven scholars. Probably the most influential version of the most influential book in history, the AV has profoundly affected the English language, contributing over 250 idioms—more even than Shakespeare. In this book, we have used the New Revised Standard Version, first released in 1989 by an ecumenical group of Christian churches in the United States, one of their aims being to produce a modern English translation free from particular theological slants.

Meaning and influence

For Jews and Christians, the Bible is considered to be divinely inspired. How this is understood varies, but it is by no means universally accepted by believers that the Bible is the "literal word of God." Indeed, the question of how to interpret the Bible is a central one for much Jewish and Christian theology. Traditionally, Christian theologians have understood there to be four senses to biblical writings—historical, allegorical, moral, and anagogical (or spiritual)—referring to different layers of meaning. Modern biblical criticism uses historical, textual, and archaeological tools and techniques of research, but most scholars also insist on the importance of literary and religious interpretations to unlock the full meaning of these rich texts.

For millions of Jews and Christians, the Bible is a constant presence, its teachings guiding their daily lives. For others, it is more remote—like the best china, used infrequently but highly cherished. It goes without saying that the importance of the Bible extends beyond those for whom it is a sacred text. It has influenced art and culture across the world and has enriched all our cultural imaginations. From great paintings and sculpture to our language itself, the Bible has shaped our lives to a significant extent; some scholars even argue that it was principles of biblical interpretation that led to the development of the methods of modern science.

The Bible is a rich treasure-house of stories and teaching that can inspire, intrigue, and offend in equal measure. For an ancient text, it has certainly lost none of its power to shock, and in this book we invite you to enter into what the great theologian Karl Barth called "the strange new world of the Bible." *Bon voyage*!

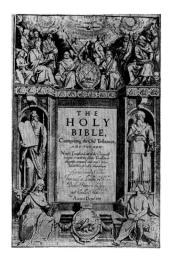

The King James Bible
Few books have had a more profound impact on the English language than the King James, or Authorized, version of the Bible. Above is the title page of the 1611 first edition.

Dead Sea scrolls
Between 1946 and 1956, 972 ancient texts—known as the Dead Sea Scrolls—were unearthed at Qumran, in what is now the West Bank. They comprise biblical, apocryphal and other documents.

IN THE BEGINNING

covenant The Hebrew word *berith*, translated as "covenant" in the Old Testament, is generally understood by scholars to mean "bond," from the root *bara*, "to bind." In the Bible, covenant refers to a binding agreement between God and his people, his blessing being promised in return for obedience. God is depicted in the Old Testament as making various such covenants, including those made with Noah (Genesis 6.11–22; 9.9–17), Abraham (Genesis 12.1–17.27; 22.15–18), and Jacob (Genesis 28.12–15), but the central covenant is that made with Moses (Exodus 19.1–24.18), the key terms of which are set out in the Ten Commandments.

Jahwist The unidentified author of various passages in the Torah (the first five books of the Bible) in which God is referred to as Yahweh instead of Elohim, the name used by the Elohist (another unidentified author of parts of the Torah).

Land of Nod All we are told of the land of Nod is that it was east of Eden. It derives from the Hebrew word meaning "to wander," and may indicate the nomadic lifestyle Cain was condemned to live as a fugitive.

New Testament Comprising the Gospels, Acts of the Apostles, various Epistles, and the book of Revelation—twenty-seven books in all, written originally in Greek—this anthology was produced in the early years of the Christian Church and is seen by Christians as the new covenant made between God and humankind through Jesus Christ.

Old Testament The first part of the Bible, this was written originally in Hebrew and comprises thirty-nine books, beginning with Genesis and ending with Malachi. Jews consider it the complete Bible, but Christians believe the New Testament is an essential second part.

Sabbath In traditional Judaism, this is the seventh day of the week, observed as a day of rest and worship to mark God's resting on the final day of creation.

tree of the knowledge of good and evil A tree in the Garden of Eden, from which Adam and Eve were barred following their expulsion. Revelation 22.2 depicts it growing in the heavenly Jerusalem, humankind finally being able to enjoy its fruits.

Yahweh Sometimes rendered Jehovah, this is a pronunciation of the Hebrew consonants YHWH, the so-called Tetragrammaton. God gives himself this name in Exodus 3.13–15. Translated as "Lord" in most biblical translations, it means, roughly, "I am who I am" and was regarded by Jews as too holy to be spoken.

The Seven Stages of Creation

Day one: Light and darkness; day and night
Day two: Sky
Day three: Dry land and sea; vegetation
Day four: Sun, moon, and stars
Day five: Sea creatures and birds
Day six: Animals and "creeping things,"
    followed by humankind
Day seven: God rests from his labors

Genesis Veterans

According to the book of Genesis, in the
early days after Creation people lived
for extraordinary lengths of time. The
following are the most remarkable:

Adam: 930 years
Seth: 912 years
Enosh: 905 years
Kenan: 910 years
Mahalel: 895 years
Jared: 962 years
Methuselah: 969 years (the oldest man
    in the Bible)
Lamech: 777 years
Noah: 950 years

The Line of Descent from Adam to Abram [1]

    Adam (*husband of Eve*)
↓ Seth (*brother of Cain and Abel*)
↓ Enosh
↓ Kenan
↓ Mahalel
↓ Jared
↓ Enoch
↓ Methusaleh
↓ Lamech
↓ Noah
↓ Shem (*brother of Ham and Japheth*)
↓ Arpachshad
↓ Shelah
↓ Eber
↓ Peleg
↓ Reu
↓ Serug
↓ Nahor
↓ Terah
↓ Abram (Abraham), (*husband of Sarah*)

[1] As recorded in Genesis. The list in Luke 3.34–38 occasionally differs slightly.

THE CREATION

the 30-second bible

The first book of the Bible starts

"in the beginning" with God's creation of heaven and earth and everything within them. The story is highly structured, with eight acts of creation over six days. On the first three days, God makes a series of divisions: the light from the dark, the waters above from the waters below, and the land from the sea. God populates these divisions in order: the land produces vegetation, lights are placed in the sky, the seas swarm with living creatures and the air is filled with birds, the land produces living creatures, and, finally, God makes humankind in His own image. Humanity is given dominion over creation, and seed-bearing plants and fruit for food—creation is vegetarian. Finally, God rests on the seventh day and blesses it, anticipating the command to observe the Sabbath as a day of rest (Exodus 20.8–11). At the end of most of the days, the phrase "And God saw that it was good" is repeated, culminating in the judgment on the sixth day that "God saw everything that He had made, and indeed, it was very good" (Genesis 1.31). The implication is clear: creation is harmonious and the world is blessed by God.

3-SECOND SERMON
God creates everything out of nothing and finds that it is very good.

3-MINUTE MEDITATION
This is the first of two creation narratives in the Bible. Known as the "Priestly," account it was probably written in the fifth century BCE and refers to God as Elohim, not Yahweh. Animals, in this account, are created before humans, and men and women are created together—both in the image of God. The story is uncompromisingly monotheistic, God creates all that is from "emptiness," there is no polytheistic struggle, and there is no account of the origin of God.

CHAPTER & VERSE
See
GENESIS 1.1–2.3

RELATED STORIES
See also
GENESIS 2.4–25
EXODUS 20.8–11
PSALM 8.3–8, 33.6–7, 95.5, 104.5–30
ISAIAH 51.9–10
2 CORINTHIANS 5.17

KEY QUOTE
In the beginning . . . God created the heavens and the earth.
GENESIS 1.1

30-SECOND TEXT
Russell Re Manning

In the beginning, says Genesis, God created the heavens and the earth, and everything within it, from a formless void, declaring all he had made to be good.

THE GARDEN OF EDEN

the 30-second bible

The Bible's second creation

narrative, known as the "Jahwist" account (due to its use of the Hebrew Yahweh, the personal name of God), begins with the creation of "a man" (*ha-adam*) from the dust of the ground (*ha-adamah*). In Genesis 1, God's act of creation is described in terms that are unique to divine creativity (the untranslatable verb *bara*, which conveys the power of "fixing destinies," is only ever used of God). By contrast, in the Jahwist account, the verb *yatsar* in "God formed man" (Genesis 2:7) is also used of a potter shaping a pot from clay. God creates a garden, called Eden (from the word for "fertility"), in the east for Adam to cultivate and fatefully instructs him not to eat from the tree of the knowledge of good and evil. God then seeks to create a "helper" for Adam and fashions the animals, which Adam names. None, however, proves a suitable partner, so God puts Adam to sleep and extracts a rib, from which He forms "a woman." The story ends with a defense of monogamous marriage—man and wife are joined together to become one flesh, naked and without shame. Ominously, however, their nakedness (*arummim*) alludes to the cunning (*arum*) of the serpent about to be introduced in the next chapter.

3-SECOND SERMON
God creates a miraculously fertile garden for Adam to tend and a wife to keep him company.

3-MINUTE MEDITATION
The story revolves around the creation of Eve, fashioned from Adam's rib. In fact, she is not named Eve until Genesis 3.20, but is referred to initially as *ishshah*, meaning "woman," a term supposedly derived from *ish*, the Hebrew word for "man," although this etymology is challenged by modern scholarship. Both names are given by Adam, who also names the animals, indicating his authority within creation, just as God's naming the elements in Genesis 1 shows His authority over creation.

CHAPTER & VERSE
See
GENESIS 2.4–25

RELATED STORIES
See also
THE CREATION
page 16
FORBIDDEN FRUIT
page 20
REVELATION 22.1–5

KEY QUOTE
And the Lord God planted a garden in Eden, in the east; and there he put the man whom he had formed.
GENESIS 2.8

30-SECOND TEXT
Russell Re Manning

The Garden of Eden was fashioned by God as a place for his most sacred creation: humankind. Here, Adam and Eve briefly experienced blissful innocence.

FORBIDDEN FRUIT

the 30-second bible

Adam and Eve may eat from any of the trees in the Garden of Eden except one: God tells Adam that if he eats the fruit of the tree of the knowledge of good and evil he will surely die. The serpent tempts Eve into eating the fruit by telling her that she will not die but instead become like God. Eve tries the fruit and gives some to Adam. The effects are dramatic: Adam and Eve become aware of their nakedness, make clothes for themselves out of fig leaves, and hide from God when they hear Him walking in the Garden. God's judgment is swift and uncompromising: the serpent is condemned to crawl on its belly and eat dust, women are condemned to pain in childbearing and subjected to their husbands, who in turn are condemned to hard agricultural labor. To prevent them from eating from the tree of life and thus achieving immortality, Adam and Eve are expelled from the Garden and the way back is barred with a flaming sword. In Christian tradition, this passage has been the basis for the doctrine of original sin; an act of disobedience that accounts for the tragic state of human existence.

3-SECOND SERMON
Adam and Eve commit the original sin and are expelled from the Garden of Eden.

3-MINUTE MEDITATION
This passage is highly ambiguous. While the snake is commonly identified with the devil, the text is enigmatic, referring to "the most crafty" of all God's creatures. Similarly, the meaning of the phrase "knowledge of good and evil" is unclear; it could mean knowledge of everything, moral awareness or sexual awakening. Although not identified, the fruit is traditionally represented as an apple, probably thanks to the similarity of the Latin words for apple and evil (*mālum* and *malum*).

CHAPTER & VERSE
See
GENESIS 3

RELATED STORIES
See also
THE TOWER OF BABEL
page 30
PENTECOST
page 140

KEY QUOTE
By the sweat of your face you shall eat bread until you return to the ground, for out of it you were taken; you are dust, and to dust you shall return.
GENESIS 3.19

30-SECOND TEXT
Russell Re Manning

The fruit of the tree of the knowledge of good and evil proved too tempting for Adam and Eve to resist, leading to their banishment from Eden in disgrace.

SATAN

Few figures in the Bible fire the popular imagination as much as Satan, commonly thought of as God's arch-opponent and the embodiment of evil. In fact, the biblical portrayal of Satan is more complex—and more mysterious.

The term "satan" is derived from the Hebrew verb meaning "to obstruct or oppose" and is primarily used with the definite article (ha-satan). Traditionally translated as "the adversary" or "the prosecutor," it is not a proper name but a title. Surprisingly, ha-satan only features in two Old Testament books: Job and Zechariah. In the book of Job, ha-satan—described as one of the "heavenly beings"—suggests that Job's faithfulness is dependent on his good fortune and that he will curse God if everything he values is taken from him. God then permits ha-satan to test Job; a challenge the accuser loses. One thing is clear in this difficult text: ha-satan is under God's control—an instrument of God's will and not an equally powerful opponent.

The other uses of Satan in the Old Testament refer to humans or angels acting as divinely inspired adversaries of Israel or her leaders. On one occasion (1 Samuel 29.4), King David is referred to as satan by the Philistines, who fear he will oppose them in battle. The most famous alleged appearance of Satan in the Old Testament—as the snake in the Garden of Eden—is not supported by the text. The serpent is simply described as the "most cunning" of the creatures (Genesis 3.1).

The New Testament is a different story. The Greek New Testament uses the term ho satanas interchangeably with ho diabolos, meaning "the slanderer," translated as "the devil." Satan has three roles in the Gospels: he tempts Jesus, possesses people, including Judas (Luke 22.3), and is invoked by the opponents of Jesus to explain Jesus' healing miracles. For Paul, Satan is an active power in the world working against the early Christians, including preventing Paul from traveling to Thessalonica (1 Thessalonians 2.18). Finally, the book of Revelation envisages an apocalyptic battle between Satan and Jesus in which, after a thousand years of confinement, Satan will be let free for a "short time" before being finally vanquished. The idea of Satan as a fallen angel is a product of later Christian theology, inspired by suggestions in the ancient Jewish, but nonbiblical work, the Book of Enoch.

The Last Judgment (altar panel, wood, late thirteenth century, by the Master of Soriguela from Vall de Ribes) shows the typical portrayal of the devil with horns and forked tail, which owes more to the medieval imagination than to the Bible. Rarely mentioned in the Old Testament, Satan in the New is portrayed as God's enemy, tempting Jesus and frustrating God's purpose, yet destined ultimately to be vanquished in a final cosmic battle.

CAIN & ABEL

the 30-second bible

The story of Adam and Eve's first two sons is both dramatic and troubling. The eldest, Cain, a crop farmer, is—ostensibly—the world's first person to be born; his younger brother, Abel, a shepherd, becomes the first to die. The root of the tragedy lies in sibling rivalry and jealousy, occasioned by God's favoring of Abel's offering of prime cuts from his flock over Cain's offering of agricultural produce. In his anger, Cain leads his brother out into a field, where he attacks and kills him. When God asks Cain where his brother is, Cain's reply is indignant: "I do not know; am I my brother's keeper?" The second part of the story relates God's punishment. Cain is cursed; the land will no longer bear crops for him and he is forced to become a restless wanderer. In response to Cain's fears that he might be attacked and killed, God places a "mark" on him, threatening vengeance seven times over upon anyone who takes his life. Cain then leaves and travels east of Eden to the land of Nod. For some, this story is symbolic of conflict between early arable and livestock farmers; others relate it to a move from hunter-gathering to fixed agricultural communities. Christians compare Abel's sacrifice and death to that of Jesus—both are portrayed as shepherds and both have their blood shed as innocent victims.

This is a story of brotherly rivalry that spills over into the world's first murder.

3-MINUTE MEDITATION
A puzzling feature of the story is Cain's fear that others will kill him, given that he is the only surviving son of Adam and Eve and thus, presumably, one of only three people alive. Perhaps he fears the wrath of his parents, although it is strange that the text does not simply say so. Genesis 5.4 refers to other sons and daughters of Adam and Eve, but these seem to be born after Seth, Adam's third son.

CHAPTER & VERSE
See
GENESIS 4.1–16

RELATED STORIES
See also
MATTHEW 23.35
HEBREWS 12.24

KEY QUOTE
Cain said to his brother Abel, "Let us go out to the field." And when they were in the field, Cain rose up against his brother Abel and killed him.
GENESIS 4.8

30-SECOND TEXT
Russell Re Manning

The world's first murder stemmed from jealousy, Cain killing his brother in a fit of rage after God preferred Abel's meat sacrifice to his own agricultural offering.

THE FLOOD

the 30-second bible

God tells the righteous Noah of His plan to destroy humanity because it had become corrupt and violent, and instructs him to build a great ship, large enough to contain two of all living creatures. For forty days and nights, the waters rise until even the highest mountains are covered and all creatures that move on the earth perish, except for those in the ark. After 150 days, God "remembers" Noah and sends a wind to disperse the waters, and the ark eventually comes to rest on Mount Ararat. To be certain the waters have abated, Noah sends out first a raven and then a dove; the latter confirms the end of the flood by returning first with a fresh olive branch and then not at all. In gratitude, Noah offers sacrifices to God, who vows never again to destroy humanity, gives Noah dominion over all creatures, and places the rainbow in the clouds as a sign of His covenant. Although narratives detailing a global inundation are common to many ancient cultures, the biblical story of the Great Flood is concerned specifically with the establishment of God's covenant with His people, and includes both a warning of divine judgment and a promise of divine protection.

3-SECOND SERMON
Resolved to destroy His creation and start again, God sends a great flood to cover the earth, sparing only the righteous Noah, his family, and two of every living thing.

3-MINUTE MEDITATION
The story of a great flood is full of telling details that suggest it was particularly linked to cultic sacrifice. For instance, Noah is instructed to take seven pairs of "clean" animals on the ark and God makes a covenant with him and his offspring in response to his sacrificial offerings after the flood has receded. Importantly, God's view of humanity does not change— humans are evil in every inclination—but Noah's faithfulness is rewarded.

CHAPTER & VERSE
See
GENESIS 6.5–9.17

RELATED STORIES
See also
MATTHEW 24.38–39
LUKE 17.27
HEBREWS 11.7
1 PETER 3.20

KEY QUOTE
And God said to Noah, "I have determined to make an end to all flesh, for the earth is filled with violence because of them; now I am going to destroy them along with the earth."
GENESIS 6.13

30-SECOND TEXT
Russell Re Manning

The subject of countless songs, poems, plays, and books, the story of the animals going two by two into the ark has long captured the public imagination.

NOAH'S CURSE

the 30-second bible

The postscript to the story of

the Flood is the peculiar and disturbing account of the fate of Noah's three sons, Shem, Ham, and Japheth. The drama begins with Noah planting the world's first vineyard. One thing leads to another: he drinks the wine, gets drunk, and lies "uncovered" in his tent. Ham, the father of Canaan, sees his father's nakedness and tells his brothers, who then, keeping their eyes averted, cover Noah with a cloak. On waking, Noah is aware of what has happened and furiously curses Ham's son, Canaan, to become the lowest of slaves to his brothers. Traditionally, the story has been interpreted as an explanation of the subjection of the Canaanites (descendants of Ham) to the Israelites (descendants of Shem and Japheth). It has also been used, unpleasantly, to justify both the institution of slavery and a variety of claims to ethnic superiority. For advocates of temperance, the story is a powerful reminder of the perils of alcohol, although commentators usually exempt Noah himself from criticism; as the first ever to drink wine, he was presumably unaware of its intoxicating effects.

3-SECOND SERMON
Discovered naked by his son, Ham, after drinking wine, Noah curses the descendants of Ham to a life of slavery.

3-MINUTE MEDITATION
The severity of Noah's reaction has led many to speculate that Ham did more than simply see his father naked. The biblical language concerning uncovering and seeing a person's nakedness may have sexual connotations, suggesting perhaps that Ham slept with Noah's wife, or even with Noah himself. Another mystery is why Noah curses Canaan and not Ham. Again, the text is ambiguous: Canaan is described as both Ham's son and as a brother to Shem and Japheth.

CHAPTER & VERSE
See
GENESIS 9.18–27

RELATED STORIES
See also
LAMENTATIONS 4.21
HABAKKUK 2.15

KEY QUOTE
Noah, a man of the soil, was the first to plant a vineyard. He drank some of the wine and became drunk, and he lay uncovered in his tent.
GENESIS 9.20–21

30-SECOND TEXT
Russell Re Manning

Graphically illustrating the pitfalls of alcohol, the curious story of Noah's inadvertent intoxication was probably intended to explain the subjection of the Canaanites to the Israelites.

THE TOWER OF BABEL

the 30-second bible

After the Flood, the descendants of Noah travel west to the land of Shinar, where they decide to settle and build a city with a tower that will reach up to the heavens. They aim to make a name for themselves and to prevent themselves from being scattered across the world. When God sees the city and its tower, He recognizes that humanity is one people with one language and that nothing they set their minds to will be impossible for them; this city and its tower are just the beginning. God's response is to confuse their language so that the people will not understand each other's speech. As a result, they are scattered across the earth and the city is left unfinished and given the name Babel, from the Hebrew *babal* meaning "jumble." For some, the confusion of languages is seen as God's punishment for humanity's pride and idolatrous ambition to overstep its rightful place by reaching to the heavens. For others, the story is more straightforwardly etiological: an explanation of the diversity of languages and cultures around the world.

3-SECOND SERMON
Noah's descendants are plunged into linguistic confusion and the great tower of Babel remains unfinished.

3-MINUTE MEDITATION
While the evidence is inconclusive, some associate the tower of Babel with "Etemenanki," the Great Ziggurat of Babylon said to have been built for Nebuchadnezzar II in the seventh century BCE. At nearly 330 feet (100 m) tall, it was called the "temple of the foundation of heaven and earth." The story of Babel has also inspired linguistic research into a single original language, the development of Esperanto, and even the fiction writer Douglas Adams' universal translator, the Babel fish.

CHAPTER & VERSE
See
GENESIS 11.1–9

RELATED STORIES
See also
FORBIDDEN FRUIT
page 20

KEY QUOTE
Come, let us go down, and confuse their language there, so that they will not understand one another's speech.
GENESIS 11.7

30-SECOND TEXT
Russell Re Manning

United after the Flood, Noah's descendants began building a mighty tower that would reach to the heavens. In response, God confused their language and scattered them across the world.

THE PROMISED LAND

Canaan The name used in the Bible for the region roughly embracing modern-day Israel, Palestine, Lebanon, and parts of Jordan and Syria. The Israelites came to see this as the Promised Land, and much of the early part of the Old Testament concerns its conquest.

manna A food miraculously provided by God to sustain the people of Israel in the wilderness (Exodus 16.14–36). Described as being "like coriander seed, white . . . the taste of it . . . like wafers made with honey" (16.31), it appeared fresh on the ground each morning. The Israelites were instructed to gather only as much as they needed to last each day; anything kept longer would immediately rot. No manna, however, was provided on the Sabbath, this being God's day of rest. Instead, He provided a double portion on the preceding day (termed Shabbat, or Preparation Day), on which they were allowed to gather sufficient to cover both.

Mount Sinai Also known in the Bible as Mount Horeb, this peak situated in a mountain range in southern Egypt is celebrated as the place where God appeared to Moses in a burning bush (see pages 46–47) and gave him the Ten Commandments (pages 52–53). Sometimes called the "Mountain of Moses" (Gebel Musa), it is held sacred by Jews, Christians, and Muslims.

Nebuchadnezzar Credited with creating the Hanging Gardens of Babylon, Nebuchadnezzar II was King of Babylon from roughly 634 to 562 BCE. The book of Daniel (3.1–30) famously tells the story of how God delivered three young Jewish men— Shadrach, Meshach, and Abednego—after the king had them thrown into a fiery furnace for refusing to worship an image he had set up. According to the Bible, as punishment for his pride, God afflicted him with insanity for seven years, during which time he reportedly ate grass like an ox (Daniel 4.33).

Passover One of the most important Jewish festivals, this celebrates how God passed over the homes of the Israelites as he brought death to the Egyptians' firstborn. Celebrated for a week each year, starting on the fifteenth day of the Jewish month of Nisan, it is also known as the feast of unleavened bread, recalling how the Israelites left Egypt in such haste that there was not even time for their dough to rise.

Patriarchs This is the collective name given to Abraham, Isaac, and Jacob (see pages 36–43), the three ancestors of the Israelites whose stories comprise the bulk of the book of Genesis. They are revered not only by Jews and Christians but also by Muslims.

The Twelve Sons of Jacob

1. Reuben (son of Leah)
2. Simeon (son of Leah)
3. Levi (son of Leah)
4. Judah (son of Leah)
5. Dan (son of Bilhah, Rachel's servant)
6. Naphtali (son of Bilhah)
7. Gad (son of Zilpah, Leah's servant)
8. Asher (son of Zilpah)
9. Issachar (son of Leah)
10. Zebulun (son of Leah)
11. Joseph (son of Rachel)
12. Benjamin (son of Rachel)

The Ten Plagues of Egypt

1. Blood
2. Frogs
3. Gnats
4. Flies
5. Pestilence
6. Boils
7. Hail and thunderstorms
8. Locusts
9. Darkness
10. Death of the firstborn

The Ten Commandments

1. You shall have no other gods before me.
2. You shall not make for yourself an idol.
3. You shall not make wrongful use of the name of the Lord your God.
4. Remember the sabbath day, and keep it holy.
5. Honor your father and your mother.
6. You shall not murder.
7. You shall not commit adultery.
8. You shall not steal.
9. You shall not bear false witness against your neighbor.
10. You shall not covet.

Women in the Bible

There are over 160 women referred to in the Bible. Here are some of the lesser-known but important women.

Deborah: ruler, judge, prophetess, and poet (Judges 4–5)

Jael: soldier and defeater of the Canaanite leader Sisera (Judges 5.31)

Rahab: prostitute spared in the destruction of Jericho (Joshua 2–6)

Tabitha: exemplar of kindness and charity raised from the dead by Peter (Acts 9.36)

Lydia: first recorded convert to Christianity in Europe (Acts 16.14)

Priscilla: wife of Aquilla who risked her life for Paul (Romans 16.3)

GOD'S PROMISE

the 30-second bible

The first of Noah's descendants to have his life told in any detail in the book of Genesis, Abram is a model of piety with whom God makes a covenant, promising to make him a father of nations, to bless his name, and to provide a homeland for his descendants. This pledge seems far-fetched: Abram's wife Sarai is barren and his household is constantly on the move, from Canaan to Egypt, then to the Negev and Bethel, and back to Canaan again. In Genesis 17, God repeats the promise, renaming Abram and Sarai as Abraham and Sarah, instructing them to call their son Isaac and establishing the rite of circumcision as the sign of membership of God's chosen people. In the following chapter, Abraham is visited by three mysterious guests, one of whom once again repeats the promise, foretelling that within a year Sarah will have a son. Sarah, who is 90 (with Abraham 100) laughs at the idea, but God's promise is fulfilled when she gives birth to Isaac. In Jewish tradition, Abraham is celebrated as "our father" who was rewarded for his trust in God in spite of adversity.

3-SECOND SERMON
God establishes a covenant with Abraham, promising to give him descendants as numerous as the stars in the sky, and land for them to live in.

3-MINUTE MEDITATION
Judaism, Christianity, and Islam all acknowledge Abraham as a founding father, hence the three collectively are known as the Abrahamic religions. For Jews, God's covenant with Abraham initiates the Jewish nation. For Christians, Abraham, who lived before God's gift of the Jewish Law to Moses, is an example of salvation through faith. In Islam, Abraham's significance lies in his firstborn son, Ishmael (whose mother was Sarah's servant Hagar), who is considered an ancestor of the Prophet Muhammad.

CHAPTER & VERSE
See
GENESIS 12.1–3; 15.1–21; 17.1–22

RELATED STORIES
See also
GENESIS 22.1–19
ROMANS 2.25–29
HEBREWS 11.8–12

KEY QUOTE
I have made you the ancestor of a multitude of nations. I will make you exceedingly fruitful; and I will make nations of you, and kings shall come from you. I will establish my covenant between me and you, and your offspring after you throughout their generations, for an everlasting covenant, to be God to you and to your offspring after you.
GENESIS 17.5–7

30-SECOND TEXT
Russell Re Manning

Told to journey to a land that God will show him, the elderly Abram is promised that all the families of the earth will be blessed through his offspring.

SODOM & GOMORRAH

the 30-second bible

3-SECOND SERMON
The cities of Sodom and Gomorrah are destroyed by God as punishment for their grave sin.

3-MINUTE MEDITATION
The nature of the "grave sin" of Sodom and Gomorrah is not specified in the biblical text, but the men's sexual desire for the angels of the lord has led many to associate the story with a condemnation of homosexuality. Sexual relations, in general, are a prominent concern in these chapters of Genesis, this story being immediately followed by the seduction of Lot by his two daughters, who both become pregnant by their father.

The story of the destruction of the cities of Sodom and Gomorrah is one of the most dramatic instances of God's wrath in the Bible. God tells Abraham about his resolve to destroy the cities on account of their sinfulness. Abraham—posing the age-old philosophical question: "Shall not the judge of all the earth do what is just?"—pleads for mercy, arguing that God would surely not kill the righteous along with the wicked. God concedes the point, promising that He will spare the cities for the sake of fifty, and finally ten, righteous men. Abraham's bargaining proves to be in vain. The two angels sent by God to Sodom are offered hospitality by Abraham's nephew, Lot, but the men of Sodom surround Lot's house and demand that he bring them out, "so that we may know them" (Genesis 19.5)— a euphemism for having sex. Their subsequent attempt to force their way in—thwarted by the angels—seals the cities' fate. God spares only Lot and his family, telling them not to look back as the two cities are destroyed by fire and brimstone from heaven. Lot's wife, however, cannot resist a final backward glance and is turned into a pillar of salt. There is no consensus on the precise location of the cities, but the story is a powerful reminder of the severity of God's righteous anger.

CHAPTER & VERSE
See
GENESIS 18.16–19.29

RELATED STORIES
See also
GENESIS 13.13
DEUTERONOMY 29.23
ISAIAH 3.9, 13.19
JEREMIAH 23.14
MATTHEW 10.15, 11.24
LUKE 10.12

KEY QUOTE
Then the Lord rained on Sodom and Gomorrah sulfur and fire from the Lord out of heaven; and he overthrew those cities, and all the Plain, and all the inhabitants of the cities, and what grew on the ground.
GENESIS 19.24–25

30-SECOND TEXT
Russell Re Manning

Unable to resist a last look at Sodom as God destroys it in punishment for its sin, Lot's wife is turned into a pillar of salt.

ABRAHAM & ISAAC

the 30-second bible

3-SECOND SERMON
God puts Abraham to the test, instructing him to sacrifice Isaac, his son.

3-MINUTE MEDITATION
The *Akedah* has had a powerful impact on Christian theologians, with many identifying the ram provided by God with Jesus Christ, and seeing Abraham's willingness to sacrifice his son as prefiguring God's. Both Isaac and Jesus carry the wood for their own sacrifice, trusting that, somehow, God will provide. A famous alternative interpretation is given by the Danish theologian Søren Kierkegaard (1813–55). In *Fear and Trembling* (1843), Kierkegaard reflects on the "absurdity" of Abraham's faith: his trust in God despite the apparent reasons not to do so.

Known in Jewish tradition as the *Akedah*, or "binding of Isaac," this story tells of Abraham's ultimate act of trust in God, who commands him to sacrifice his son, Isaac, on a mountaintop in Moriah. On reaching the mountain, Abraham leaves behind his two servants and goes up alone with Isaac, on whom he places the wood for the burned offering. When Isaac asks what they will use as the sacrifice, Abraham replies that God will provide; shortly afterward he binds Isaac on the top of the pyre and takes up his knife ready to kill his son. At the last moment, Abraham is stopped by the voice of the Lord's angel telling him not to lay a hand on the boy. Looking up, he finds a ram caught in a thicket by its horns, which he sacrifices instead. The angel speaks a second time, blessing Abraham for not having withheld his son. The story is stark in its simplicity, illustrating the extent of Abraham's absolute faith in God, although interpreters disagree over whether Abraham's confidence is that God will somehow spare Isaac or will fulfill His covenant by some other means.

CHAPTER & VERSE
See
GENESIS 22.1–19

RELATED STORIES
See also
HEBREWS 11.17–19

KEY QUOTE
Do not lay your hand on the boy or do anything to him; for now I know that you fear God, since you have not withheld your son, your only son, from me.
GENESIS 22.12

30-SECOND TEXT
Russell Re Manning

Satisfied that Abraham is willing to offer even his son Isaac, God sends an angel to stop him, and provides a ram to sacrifice instead.

JACOB & ESAU

the 30-second bible

3-SECOND SERMON
This is a tale of sibling rivalry between Isaac's twin sons, as Jacob twice tricks Esau.

3-MINUTE MEDITATION
Brotherly rivalry is a frequent theme in the narratives of the book of Genesis, from Cain and Abel, to Jacob and Esau, to Jacob's twelve sons. This reflects the nature of the narrative, an extended family tree of the Jewish people. Like any family, the Israelites have their fair share of family feuds, disgraced relatives, and dramatic reconciliations. Unlike other families, however, the history of Israel is dominated by their relations with God—a constant presence in the lives of the Patriarchs.

Abraham's son Isaac marries

Rebekah, a woman from Abraham's father's country, and she conceives twin sons, who jostle with each other in her womb. God tells her that she carries two nations within her and that the older will serve the younger. This prophecy is realized when the elder, Esau, a ruddy and hairy man, is twice tricked by the younger, Jacob, who was born clutching his brother's heel (a Hebrew idiom for deception). First, Esau, tired after a day's hunting, sells his birthright to Jacob for a bowl of lentil soup. Second, Jacob tricks his father, Isaac—now blind in old age—into blessing him instead of Esau by wearing his brother's clothes and covering his smooth hands and neck with goatskin. To escape Esau's vengeful anger, Jacob, with the assistance of his mother, persuades his father to send him away to seek a wife from Rebekah's family. Throughout the narrative, Jacob is helped by Rebekah, while Isaac clearly prefers his elder son. The two brothers are eventually reconciled, both having prospered in the meantime. On the night before their reconciliation, Jacob wrestles with a stranger—none other, it turns out, than God—who blesses Jacob and renames him Israel, probably meaning "he struggles with God." In spite of his trickery, Jacob is blessed and becomes the father of the twelve tribes of the nation of Israel.

CHAPTER & VERSE
See
GENESIS 25.19–34;
26.34–28.5; 32.3–33.20

RELATED STORIES
See also
THE PRODIGAL SON
page 120

KEY QUOTE
Esau said, "Is he not rightly named Jacob? For he has supplanted me these two times. He took away my birthright; and look, now he has taken away my blessing."
GENESIS 27.36

30-SECOND TEXT
Russell Re Manning

Despite cheating his brother Esau out of his inheritance, Jacob secures God's blessing after daring to wrestle with him and becomes the founding father of Israel.

THE PHARAOH'S DREAMS

the 30-second bible

3-SECOND SERMON
Joseph interprets the Pharaoh's dreams, demonstrating the power of God and in the process rising to prominence in Egypt.

3-MINUTE MEDITATION
Dreams and their interpretation are a central theme in many Old Testament passages, including Jacob's dream of a ladder ascending into heaven and Daniel's interpretation of Nebuchadnezzar's dream of a statue with feet of clay. Joseph and Daniel's ability to interpret dreams is compared to the impotence of pagan astrologers and magicians. Both Joseph and Daniel, however, insist that correct interpretation comes not from them but from God, dreams being prophetic messages sent by Him.

Of Jacob's twelve sons, it is the eleventh, Joseph, to whom most attention is devoted. His father's favorite, nicknamed "the dreamer," Joseph is sold into slavery by his brothers after he dreams of his family bowing down before him. Once in Egypt, Joseph prospers, but after piously rejecting his master's wife's advances finds himself in prison. There, he correctly interprets the dreams of two of Pharaoh's jailed officials, so when the Pharaoh subsequently has two disturbing dreams—one of seven lean cows coming out of the Nile and eating seven fat cows, and the other of seven withered ears of grain devouring seven full ears of grain—Joseph's help is called upon. Joseph correctly interprets the dreams as foretelling seven years of plenty to be followed by seven years of famine, and recommends storing up a fifth of the harvest in the good years to get the Egyptians through the ensuing crisis. A grateful Pharaoh appoints Joseph as vizier in charge of "all the land of Egypt" (Genesis 41.41). Like so many in Genesis, Joseph's story is one of triumph over adversity; a reminder that although God's people may suffer along the way, their faithfulness will be rewarded.

CHAPTER & VERSE
See
GENESIS 40.1–41.57

RELATED STORIES
See also
GENESIS 28.11–17
DANIEL 2.1–49
AMOS 3.7

KEY QUOTE
Pharaoh said to Joseph, "I have had a dream, and there is no one who can interpret it. I have heard it said of you that when you hear a dream you can interpret it." Joseph answered Pharaoh, "It is not I; God will give Pharaoh a favorable answer."
GENESIS 41.15–16

30-SECOND TEXT
Russell Re Manning

The Pharaoh's dreams baffle his diviners, but Joseph, guided by God, interprets them as foretelling seven years of plenty followed by seven of famine.

THE BURNING BUSH

the 30-second bible

While tending his father-in-law's flock of sheep, Moses sees a bush in flames yet not being burned up. As he goes to investigate, he hears the voice of God speaking to him from the bush. Told to remove his sandals as he is standing on holy ground, Moses turns his face away, afraid to look at God. God then instructs him that he will lead the Israelites from slavery in Egypt to freedom in Canaan—the land promised to Abraham and now described as flowing with milk and honey. God tells Moses that He has seen and heard the suffering of His people and will compel the Egyptians to let the Israelites go free. In a mix of self-effacement and daring, Moses asks God who he should say has sent him and how he should respond if the Israelites refuse to believe him. God replies that He is the God of their ancestors—Abraham, Isaac, and Jacob—and that he will perform wonders to convince the Jewish people. As a foretaste, God transforms Moses' staff into a serpent before withering and then healing his hand. Throughout this narrative and the story of the liberation from Egypt that follows it, God's power over nature is a central theme—from the bush itself and the miraculous transformations to God's angry riposte, when Moses pleads for someone more eloquent to be sent in his place, that speech and sight come from Him alone.

3-SECOND SERMON
God reveals Himself to Moses in a burning bush and commissions him to bring the Israelites out of Egypt.

3-MINUTE MEDITATION
The story of the burning bush contains one of the most important theological texts in the whole Bible. Moses asks God's name and in reply God says "Ehyeh-Asher-Ehyer," usually translated as "I am who I am" although some scholars prefer "I will be what I will be." Probably related to the Tetragrammaton (YHWH), this is considered both a personal name of God and a theological definition identifying God as both ineffable and the transcendent source of all being.

CHAPTER & VERSE
See
EXODUS 3.1–4.17

RELATED STORIES
See also
DEUTERONOMY 32.39
ISAIAH 48.12
JOHN 4.26, 8.28, 58
ACTS 7.36–41

KEY QUOTE
Moses said to God, "If I come to the Israelites and say to them, 'The God of your ancestors has sent me to you,' and they ask me, 'What is his name?' what shall I say to them?" God said to Moses, "I am who I am." He said further, "Thus you shall say to the Israelites, 'I am has sent me to you.'"
EXODUS 3.13–14

30-SECOND TEXT
Russell Re Manning

Seeing a bush that, although burning, is not consumed by the flames, Moses realizes that he is in the very presence of God.

MOSES

A central figure in the Old

Testament, Moses is associated with some of the key moments in the biblical narrative, from God's self-revelation in the burning bush and the exodus from Egypt, to the gift of the Ten Commandments and the entry of the Israelites into the Promised Land. Traditionally considered the author of the first five books of the Old Testament (known as the Torah in Judaism), more than any other biblical figure Moses is representative of the Old Testament ideal of law-abiding fidelity. In both Christianity and Islam, Moses is a revered figure; he is the Old Testament character that is most frequently mentioned in the New Testament and the Qur'an and is often compared to Jesus and Muhammad.

Moses' life story encapsulates the history of the Israelites. Born into slavery in Egypt, he is hidden in a basket by his mother, Jochebed, among the rushes of the Nile River (Exodus 2.1–3) after the Pharaoh commands all newborn Hebrew boys should be killed. Moses is found by the Pharaoh's daughter and brought up within the royal household (with his birth mother as wet nurse). After killing an Egyptian whom he sees beating a Hebrew, Moses spends forty years as a shepherd in Midian before being summoned by God to return to Egypt to liberate his people, who he then leads through the desert for another forty years before dying on a mountaintop overlooking the Promised Land. He is said to have been buried by God Himself. Throughout the narrative of the exodus from Egypt and wandering in the desert, Moses has a lively relationship with the Jewish people, who repeatedly complain about their situation and require a constant combination of miraculous interventions and judicial justice to keep them united.

Moses' primary importance lies in his founding the nation of Israel by communicating God's gift of the Law through the Ten Commandments. Known in Jewish tradition as the Lawgiver, he is credited with establishing Judaism's distinctive ethical monotheism—based on the direct commandments of God—and its priestly hierarchy as the means of securing His people's adherence to the Law. It is this unflinching faith in God's justice, rather than his greatness as a leader or the miracles he performed, that defines Moses' significance.

Although Moses features in some of the most dramatic stories in the Old Testament—including the burning bush, the plagues of Egypt, and the crossing of the Red Sea—Moses is perhaps most associated with God's giving of the Ten Commandments on Mount Sinai. Not for nothing is the Jewish Law also known as the Law of Moses.

THE EXODUS

the 30-second bible

3-SECOND SERMON
Moses leads the Israelites out of Egypt and into the desert on their quest for the Promised Land.

3-MINUTE MEDITATION
The story of the Exodus is full of ritual and symbolic significance, centered on the important Jewish festival of Passover (Pesach), the name of which recalls how God spared the Israelites by passing over their houses. Celebrated by Jewish believers to this day, it is seen by Christians as a precursor to the Lord's Supper—the new Passover—through which they remember the sacrificial death of Jesus.

Having already sent nine plagues upon Egypt, God tells every Israelite family, via Moses, to slaughter a lamb, celebrate a ritual meal, and smear the doorframes of their houses with the lambs' blood so that He will know to spare them from the most devastating plague of all: the death of every firstborn in Egypt. When this strikes that very night, the distraught Pharaoh commands the Israelites to leave. They do so in such haste that the dough for their bread does not have time to rise, journeying into the desert guided by a pillar of cloud in the day and of fire by night. The departure from Egypt is just the first step in the Israelites' long journey to the Promised Land, and they endure many hardships along the way, provoking the recurring lament: "Was it because there were no graves in Egypt that you have taken us away to die in the wilderness?" Moses repeatedly calls on them to stand firm and trust God, who performs a series of miracles of deliverance—the waters of the Red Sea part, manna falls from heaven, and Moses brings water forth from a rock. An archetypal story of a people's dramatic liberation, the Exodus narratives place great stress on the importance of remembering—just as God remembered the suffering of his people, so too they are enjoined to remember His mercy.

CHAPTER & VERSE
See
EXODUS 12.1–19.25

RELATED STORIES
See also
THE BURNING BUSH
page 46
MOSES
page 48

KEY QUOTE
They baked unleavened cakes of the dough that they had brought out of Egypt; it was not leavened, because they were driven out of Egypt and could not wait, nor had they prepared any provisions for themselves.
EXODUS 12.39

30-SECOND TEXT
Russell Re Manning

Set free from slavery in Egypt after a succession of plagues, the Israelites were subsequently delivered from their pursuers after God parted the waters of the Red Sea.

THE TEN COMMANDMENTS

the 30-second bible

3-SECOND SERMON
Moses receives the gift of the Law from God, divinely inscribed on two stone tablets.

3-MINUTE MEDITATION
The Ten Commandments have an ambiguous place in Christianity. For Christians, Jesus' teachings replace those of Moses, as summed up in Jesus' so-called Great Commandment (actually two commandments) to "love the Lord your God with all your heart, and with all your soul, and with all your mind" and to "love your neighbor as yourself" (Matthew 22.37, 39). At the same time, many Protestant churches prominently display the two tablets of the Law, preferring the Word of God to any potentially idolatrous images.

On the third day after arriving at Mount Sinai, the Israelites witness thunder and lightning and hear the sound of a trumpet from within a dark cloud on the mountain. Moses goes up the mountain to meet with God, who speaks to him directly, issuing ten commandments, comprising instructions to worship only God, to keep the Sabbath, and to honor parents, and prohibitions on idolatry, blasphemy, murder, adultery, theft, false testimony, and coveting a neighbor's household or belongings. The commandments—which were later inscribed directly onto two stone tablets by "the finger of God" (Exodus 24.12, 31.18)—are written in a strikingly terse style, and form the basis of the Jewish Law. Further details of the Law are spelled out to Moses by God, including comprehensive instructions concerning the Tabernacle, the portable "dwelling place" for the divine presence, and the Ark of the Covenant, a chest containing the stone tablets and other holy items. God subsequently provides a second set of tablets for the Ark after Moses smashes the originals upon discovering the Israelites dancing around an idolatrous statue of a golden calf. For Jews, the gift of the Law is central to Jewish religion and, traditionally, the Ten Commandments were recited daily as reminders of the obligations of the faithful.

CHAPTER & VERSE
See
EXODUS 19.16–20.17

RELATED STORIES
See also
DEUTERONOMY 5.4–21
MATTHEW 22.35–40
MARK 12.28–34
LUKE 10.25–28
ROMANS 13.8–10

KEY QUOTE
You shall have no other gods before me.
EXODUS 20.3

30-SECOND TEXT
Russell Re Manning

God inscribed the Ten Commandments onto tablets of stone not once, but twice, Moses having furiously smashed the first set on discovering the Israelites worshipping an idol.

BIBLICAL HISTORY

ark (of the Covenant) A portable chest, or tabernacle, the making of which is described in the book of Exodus, created at God's command to house the stone tablets on which were inscribed the Ten Commandments (see pages 52–53). It was carried by priests ahead of the people throughout the long years of the Exodus (see pages 50–51) and in their conquest of the Promised Land.

Malachi The last of the twelve so-called minor prophets, Malachi exercised his prophetic ministry around 450 BCE. In the book bearing his name, he challenges the people of Judah concerning social injustice and religious laxity, warning that, as a result, God will come to punish instead of bless them.

Moab A region west of Judah, separated from the latter by the Jordan River and Red Sea. In biblical times, there was frequent conflict between Israelites and Moabites.

Philistines A tribe from the region of Philistia bordering ancient Israel to the east, the Philistines are portrayed in the Old Testament as bitter enemies of the Israelites.

Saul Appointed by popular demand as the first king of Israel, Saul ruled for around twenty years. He was eventually killed, together with three of his sons, in a battle against the Philistines.

Judges of Israel

After the death of Joshua, the following served as leaders of the Israelites up until the time of Saul, their first king:

Othniel 1377–1337 BCE[1] (Judges 3.9–11)
Ehud 1319–1240 BCE (Judges 3.15–30)
Shamgar 1260–1250 BCE (Judges 3.31)
Deborah 1240–1200 BCE (Judges 4.4–5.13)
Gideon 1193–1153 BCE (Judges 6.11–8.35)[2]
Tola 1150–1127 BCE (Judges 10.1–2)
Jair 1127–1105 BCE (Judges 10.3–5)
Jephthah 1087–1081 BCE (Judges 11.1–12.7)
Ibzan 1081–1073 BCE (Judges 12.8–10)
Elon 1073–1063 BCE (Judges 12.11–12)
Abdon 1063–1056 BCE (Judges 12.13–15)
Samson 1076–1055 BCE (Judges 13.2–16.31)
Eli dates uncertain (1 Samuel 1.9, 12–18, 2.11, 20–3.14, 4.13–18)
Samuel dates uncertain (1 Samuel 1.20–25.1, 28.3, 11–20)

Kings of Israel and Judah

Saul 1050–1010 BCE (1 Samuel 9.1–31.13; 1 Chronicles 10.1–14)
David 1010–970 BCE (1 Samuel 16.11–30.31; 2 Samuel 1.1–24.25; 1 Kings 1.1–2.11; 1 Chronicles 10.14–29.30)
Solomon 970–930 BCE (1 Kings 1.39–11.43; 1 Chronicles 29.21–25, 28; 2 Chronicles 1.1–9.31)

1 All dates are approximate.
2 One of Gideon's sons, Abimelech, declared himself king, "ruling" there for three years (Judges 9.1–57).

Kings of Israel[3]

Jeroboam 930–909 BCE (1 Kings 12.20–14.201)
Nadab 909–909 BCE (1 Kings 15.25–26)
Baasha 908–886 BCE (1 Kings 15.27–16.7)
Elah 886–885 BCE (1 Kings 16.8–10)
Zimri 885 BCE (1 Kings 16.9–20)
Omri 885–874 BCE (1 Kings 16.16, 21–28)[4]
Ahab 874–853 BCE (1 Kings 16.29–22.40)
Ahaziah 853–852 BCE (1 Kings 22.51–53;
    2 Kings 1.1–18)
Jehoram (also called Joram) 852–841 BCE
    (2 Kings 1.17, 3.1–12, 9.14–24)
Jehu 841–814 BCE (2 Kings 9–14–10.36)
Jehoahaz (Samaria) 814–798 BCE
    (2 Kings 13.1–9)
Jehoash 798–782 BCE (2 Kings 13.10–13,
    14.11–16)
Jeroboam II 793–753 BCE (2 Kings 14.16, 23–29)
Zechariah 753 BCE (2 Kings 14.29, 15.8–12)
Shallum 752 BCE (2 Kings 15.13–15)
Menahem 793–753 BCE (2 Kings 15.16–22)
Pekahiah 742–740 BCE (2 Kings 15.22–26)
Pekah 752–732 BCE (1 Kings 15.27–32)
Hoshea 732–722 BCE (2 Kings 17.1–4)

Kings (and Queen) of Judah

Rehoboam 933–916 BCE (1 Kings 14.21–31)
Abijam 915–913 BCE (1 Kings 14.31–15.8)
Asa 912–872 BCE (1 Kings 15.8–24)
Jehoshaphat 874–850 BCE
    (1 Kings 15.24, 22.1–50)
Jehoram (also called Joram) 850–843 BCE
    (1 Kings 22.50; 2 Kings 8.16–24)
Ahaziah 843 BCE (2 Kings 8.25–29, 9.16,
    21–29)
Athaliah (Queen of Judah, wife of Jehoram)
    843–837 BCE (2 Kings 11.1)
Joash (also called Jehoash) 843–803 BCE
    (2 Kings 11.21–12.21)
Amaziah 803–775 BCE (2 Kings 12.21, 14.1–15,
    17–20)
Azariah (also called Uzziah) 787–735 BCE
    (2 Kings 14.21, 15.1–8, 17, 23, 27, 30)
Jotham 749–734 BCE (2 Kings 15.30–38)
Ahaz 741–726 BCE (2 Kings 15.38–16.20)
Hezekiah 726–697 BCE (2 Kings 18.1–21)
Manasseh 697–642 BCE (2 Kings 20.21–21.18)
Amon 641–640 BCE (2 Kings 21.18–26)
Josiah 639–608 BCE (2 Kings 21.26–23.30)
Jehoahaz 608 BCE (2 Kings 23.30–34)
Jehoiakim 608–597 BCE (2 Kings 23.34–24.6)
Jehoiachin 597 BCE (2 Kings 24.6, 8–17,
    25.27–30)
Zedekiah 597–586 BCE (2 Kings 24.17–25.7)

3 During David's reign, Ishbosheth—the fourth son of
Saul—proclaimed himself king of Israel. A two-year civil war
ensued until Ishbosheth was murdered by two of his captains.
Later, Jeroboam and Rehoboam—the two sons of Solomon—
vied for the throne and the country was divided into a
northern kingdom, which retained the name Israel, and
southern kingdom, Judah.
4 2 Chronicles 9.31–36.13 also give details of the various
rulers of Israel and Judah.

5 After Zimri usurped the throne, Tibni, son of Ginath, vied
for power with Omri (1 Kings 16.21–22) until Omri finally
emerged victorious.

THE WALLS
OF JERICHO

the 30-second bible

After Moses dies, Joshua leads

Israel's conquest of the Promised Land. Around
1400 BCE, the Israelites enter Canaan by
miraculously crossing the Jordan, only to find
themselves faced by the walled and barricaded
city of Jericho. Following divine instruction,
Israelite warriors and seven priests, each
trumpeting a ram's horn and preceding God's
ark, march once around the city on six
successive days. The next day, they march
around it seven times and then the people—
having hitherto been silent—mightily shout,
whereupon, the walls collapse—as promised
by God—and the Israelites fall upon the city,
slaughtering every person and beast. Only
the household of Rahab, a prostitute who had
earlier saved Israelite spies and paid homage
to Israel's God, is spared. Obeying God's further
stipulations, no booty is taken, everything being
burned apart from precious metals, which are
put into the Lord's treasury. However, when
the Israelites are subsequently defeated in battle
by the Amorites, it emerges that one man—
Achan—has disobeyed God's instructions. For
this, he is stoned to death. Israel's steadfast
adherence to God's commands, in contrast
to Achan's disobedience, exemplifies faith in
action. The story also illustrates Israel's total
dependence on God's guidance and blessing.

3-SECOND SERMON
God brings down the
walls of Jericho after the
Israelites faithfully follow
divine instructions.

3-MINUTE MEDITATION
Slaying every living being
in Jericho, including
children, has troubled
many a reader. Three
biblical reasons suggest
themselves. First,
destruction of the
Canaanites would prevent
religious contamination by
their detestable practices,
such as child sacrifice.
Second, the Canaanites'
perpetual degradation had,
since Abraham, reached a
point that required God's
judgment. Third, parents'
sin affects their offspring.
Jericho's destruction was,
therefore, not immoral;
its cause was. Sin causes
death, but repentance, like
Rahab's, restores to life.

CHAPTER & VERSE
See
JOSHUA 6.1–7.26

RELATED STORIES
See also
DEUTERONOMY 20.16–18
JOSHUA 2.1–24, 24.11–13
PSALM 108.12–13
HEBREWS 11.29–31

KEY QUOTE
So the people shouted, and the
trumpets were blown. As soon
as the people heard the sound
of the trumpets, they raised
a great shout, and the wall
fell down flat; so the people
charged straight ahead into the
city and captured it.
JOSHUA 6.20

30-SECOND TEXT
Stefan Bosman

*As the seven priests
blew their trumpets
and the people of Israel
shouted out, the walls
of Jericho came crashing
down before them.*

SAMSON & DELILAH

the 30-second bible

Blessed with superhuman

strength, Samson—who has never drunk wine or cut his hair—has long been vexing the Philistines. They finally see a chance to bring him down when he falls for a Philistine woman, Delilah. Allured with copious amounts of silver, she tries to unlock the secret to his extraordinary strength, persistently begging Samson to tell her. Three times he fabricates explanations, before finally revealing that being shaved will make him a normal man. When he subsequently falls asleep in her lap, Samson's seven locks are shaved off and, for the first time, he is powerless against the Philistines, who burst in upon him, gouge out his eyes, and force him into hard manual labor. Later, during a festival of the Philistine god Dagon, the Philistine lords bring Samson out for sport into a packed building where thousands have gathered to celebrate. Praying to God for a final bestowal of strength, he places his hands on the central two columns and brings down the roof upon them all, killing more Philistines in this final sacrificial act than ever before. Although the wiles of an exotic female seem responsible for rendering this extraordinary warrior helpless, closer scrutiny reveals that the real cause was his own pride. He had started to believe in his own strength instead of its true source, God (Judges 15.16, 16.20).

3-SECOND SERMON
Samson, an Israelite hero unmatched in physical strength, is rendered helpless after his wife, Delilah, wheedles out of him the secret of his awesome power.

3-MINUTE MEDITATION
Following the Israelite conquest of Canaan, judges periodically arose to deliver the Israelites from foreign oppression, which had resulted from Israel's apostasy. Samson—one such leader—was no different than whimsical Israel. Divinely bestowed with superhuman strength, he neglected God and boasted in himself. Yet strong parallels exist between Samson and Jesus in their divinely announced births, their saving of Israel, their being temporarily forsaken by God, and their triumphing through sacrificial death.

CHAPTER & VERSE
See
JUDGES 16.4–31

RELATED STORIES
See also
JUDGES 13.1–16.4
NEHEMIAH 13.23–27
HEBREWS 11.32–34

KEY QUOTE
Then she said, "The Philistines are upon you, Samson!" When he awoke from his sleep, he thought, "I will go out as at other times, and shake myself free." But he did not know that the Lord had left him.
JUDGES 16.20

30-SECOND TEXT
Stefan Bosman

Was it the lure of 1,100 pieces of silver or simply the prospect of humiliating the scourge of the Philistines that led Delilah to betray her lover, Samson?

RUTH & BOAZ

the 30-second bible

The book of Ruth is a kind of morality play, with idealized characters who display true friendship within the context of Israelite law and who play a key role as ancestors of King David. Naomi is an Israelite widow in the foreign land of Moab. When her two sons die prematurely, she tells her Moabite daughters-in-law to return to their family homes, but the faithful Ruth promises that she will never leave her: "your people shall be my people, and your God my God." They travel to Bethlehem, and go to the home of Naomi's kinsman Boaz, who shows great kindness to Ruth. Naomi advises her one night to bathe and anoint herself, in order to present herself as a suitable partner to Boaz. Ruth goes to him and asks for his protection, under the law of levirate marriage by which the kin of a dead husband is to care for his widow and property. Boaz promises that if her closest kinsman does not accept this duty, he will do so instead. When the other kinsman declines, Boaz marries her, and Ruth eventually gives birth to a son, Obed. Naomi rejoices at her new grandson who, we learn, will become the grandfather of King David. The eventual marriage of Ruth and Boaz shows God's providential work by means of mutual love, ultimately leading to the birth of Israel's greatest king.

3-SECOND SERMON
A foreign woman, Ruth, shows exemplary filial piety toward her mother-in-law, is blessed with marriage to Boaz, and becomes great-grandmother to King David.

3-MINUTE MEDITATION
The book of Ruth is a noble tale of friendship and self-sacrifice. The relationship between Naomi and the foreign woman Ruth is beautiful, both seeking the good of the other. Boaz, too, is a character of great honor and compassion, caring for his kinswoman and her daughter-in-law.

CHAPTER & VERSE
See
RUTH 1.1–4.22

RELATED STORIES
See also
LEVITICUS 25.25
DEUTERONOMY 25.5–10

KEY QUOTE
Where you go, I will go; where you lodge, I will lodge; your people shall be my people, and your God my God.
RUTH 1.16

30-SECOND TEXT
Tim Muldoon

A supreme example of faithfulness and great-grandmother to King David—surely an Israelite woman of the highest credentials? But no, Ruth instead was a refugee from Moab.

DAVID & GOLIATH
the 30-second bible

3-SECOND SERMON
A young shepherd, David, faces a giant warrior, Goliath, in single combat, but the apparent underdog, David, prevails.

3-MINUTE MEDITATION
The story is not just about a boy and a giant. Rather, it is steeped in religious conflict. Thus, Goliath taunts not just an army, but God's army. Goliath invokes his pagan gods against David. David counters by going out against Goliath in the name of the Lord. The foe falls like Dagon, a Philistine deity, had earlier fallen before God's ark (1 Samuel 5.3–4).

In the eleventh century BCE, the Philistines gathered to attack the Israelites in Elah Valley, southwest of Jerusalem. Instead of engaging their foe, however, the Philistines presented a champion, Goliath—an impressive warrior reportedly 9 feet 10 inches (3 meters) tall—who, every morning and evening for forty days, challenged the Israelites to present a champion of their own to decide the battle. The whole of Israel cowered before Goliath, except for a young shepherd called David, who, infuriated by Goliath's taunts, pleaded with King Saul to let him fight the Philistine. Hesitantly, given David's youth and inexperience, Saul agrees. Mocking and cursing David, Goliath declares that he will give his flesh to the birds and animals, but David confidently responds that God will give him the victory instead. When the battle begins, Goliath wields a javelin, spear, and sword, whereas David has only a staff, sling, and five stones. Approaching Goliath, David slings the first stone into the Philistine's forehead and he collapses. Quickly taking Goliath's sword, David beheads him, whereupon the Israelites proceed to rout the Philistines. David's courageous act made him a hero of faith, exemplifying the conviction that when one trusts in the Lord, one can face any godly challenge, no matter how great.

CHAPTER & VERSE
See
1 SAMUEL 17.1–58

RELATED STORIES
See also
1 SAMUEL 5.3–4, 21.8–9, 22.9–10
PSALM 20.7
HEBREWS 11.32–34

KEY QUOTE
You come to me with sword and spear and javelin; but I come to you in the name of the Lord of hosts.
1 SAMUEL 17.45

30-SECOND TEXT
Stefan Bosman

A young shepherd versus a mighty Philistine warrior, seemingly no contest, yet in one of the most memorable giant-killing tales of all time, David triumphs against the odds.

DAVID & BATHSHEBA

the 30-second bible

3-SECOND SERMON
A tale of adultery, the story of David and Bathsheba is about power, lust, sin, its consequences, and, ultimately, God's forgiveness.

3-MINUTE MEDITATION
Psalm 51, known as the "Miserere" ("Have mercy") in Latin, one of the most frequently used penitential psalms, is described as a psalm of David composed when Nathan came to him after his affair with Bathsheba. It is a profound meditation on the corrosive effects of sin on one's heart. It reflects the reality that even the king of Israel, the one favored by God, can fall into sin.

David, the great king of Israel, spies a beautiful woman bathing while he is walking along the roof of the palace. Despite being told she is married to Uriah, he sends messengers to fetch her and makes love to her. When Bathsheba soon afterward tells David she is pregnant, he attempts to cover his sin by recalling Uriah from battle, but Uriah, a model of duty, refuses to sleep with his wife at home while his comrades are at war. So David instead arranges for Uriah to be in the front line during battle, and Uriah is killed. When Bathsheba learns of Uriah's death, she mourns. But, after the prescribed period of mourning, David summons her to his house and marries her. Bathsheba bears a son. God calls the prophet Nathan to confront David with the enormity of his sin, prophesying that David's house will always be at war and that his neighbor will lie with his wives in broad daylight. David repents, but Nathan tells him that although God has forgiven him, he will nevertheless punish him by killing his son. In time, Absalom, David's son by another woman, fulfills both of the prophecies in his war against David. The story of David and Bathsheba illustrates that even though God chooses imperfect people to fulfill his plans, still God's justice and mercy will prevail in the end.

CHAPTER & VERSE
See
2 SAMUEL 11.1–12.25

RELATED STORIES
See also
2 SAMUEL 15:1–19:43
PSALM 51

KEY QUOTE
It happened, late one afternoon, when David rose from his couch and was walking about on the roof of the king's house, that he saw from the roof a woman bathing; the woman was very beautiful . . . So David sent messengers to get her, and she came to him, and he lay with her.
2 SAMUEL 11:2, 4a

30-SECOND TEXT
Tim Muldoon

A nude woman bathing, and one thing leads to another, David setting in motion a train of events that will haunt him for the rest of his life.

SOLOMON'S WISDOM

the 30-second bible

3-SECOND SERMON
God invites Solomon to ask of Him anything; to God's delight, Solomon asks for wisdom—the wisdom to rule with justice and righteousness.

3-MINUTE MEDITATION
The wisdom books stress that genuine wisdom is rooted in the "fear of the Lord," the transcendent source of wisdom. Further, the wisdom literature is inherently transcultural in its message and concern. Biblical wisdom also seeks a change of heart from within, an integral transformation of character. These three characteristics, then, capture the tenor of biblical wisdom: transcendent in its source; transcultural in its scope and reach; and transformational in its life-changing effects.

God appears to King Solomon in a vision, offering him anything his heart desires; Solomon requests not long life and riches, but wisdom. Two harlots then approach Solomon, disputing over a baby that each claims to be her own. Solomon's proposed solution is to cut the baby in two: half of the child will go to one woman, and half to the other. Upon hearing the decision, the true mother cries out in horror; at once, Solomon knows the identity of the rightful mother and rules accordingly. The wisdom of Solomon displayed here finds literary expression in the "wisdom books" of the Bible (Proverbs, Ecclesiastes, Job, Psalms, Song of Solomon). A remarkable feature of these books is their often intentional move away from Israelite-specific concerns, such as sacrificial ritual and the like, to universal concerns, such as justice and righteousness, the problem of human suffering, and taking care of the poor and needy. In part, this reflects the fact that for a brief period the kingdom of David and Solomon had truly international aspirations; other nations were coming to Jerusalem to hear the wisdom of Solomon. God's gift of wisdom to Solomon fostered this very development, making it possible to teach the nations in a universal language they could understand.

CHAPTER & VERSE
See
1 KINGS 3.1–14, 16–28, 4.29–34

RELATED STORIES
See also
JOB 28.28
PSALM 1.1–6, 111.10
PROVERBS 1.7
ECCLESIASTES 12.13

KEY QUOTE
The fear of the Lord is the beginning of wisdom.
PROVERBS 9.10

30-SECOND TEXT
Andrew D. Swafford

Two women, one baby—but which is the true mother? Solomon's solution to this harrowing conundrum perfectly illustrates his fabled wisdom.

ELIJAH

Elijah, whose name means

"Yahweh is my God" and whose story is told predominantly in the books of Kings, is one of the major Old Testament prophets. His message consistently emphasizes the importance of a strict interpretation of Mosaic Law, especially its absolute insistence upon the exclusive worship of Yahweh alone. He was active in the Northern Kingdom of Israel during the reign of King Ahab, who in order to secure peace and economic prosperity had reverted to pre-Mosaic religious practices and permitted the worship of the Canaanite fertility god Baal, even marrying Jezebel, a priestess of Baal. Elijah, dubbed by Ahab "the troubler of Israel," is unsparing in his condemnation of Ahab and Jezebel and announces a great drought sent by God—so severe that not even dew will form. When the prophets of Baal entreat their god to end the drought, Elijah pitilessly mocks their failure before successfully calling on God for rain.

Elijah is the subject of two profound and touching stories. In the first story, he is given refuge and food by a widowed mother in Zarephath. When the widow's son dies, Elijah calls on God to restore him to life in order to demonstrate the trustworthiness of God's word. The boy is restored to life and the widow praises God, in contrast to Ahab's unbelief. Some time later, Elijah journeys to Mount Horeb (otherwise called Sinai), where Moses received the Ten Commandments (see pages 52–53). The first to retrace Moses' steps, Elijah laments to God that he is the only faithful one left among the Israelites. He listens for the voice of the Lord, and a great wind comes, but God is not in it, nor in a great earthquake, nor in a great fire. Finally, in the words of the King James Version, Elijah heard the "still small voice" (1 Kings 19.12) of God entrusting him with his prophetic mission.

According to 2 Kings 11, Elijah does not die, but is taken up into heaven in a chariot of fire (see pages 72–73), leading to the belief that he will return at the *eschaton*, or end of time. In Jewish tradition, a place is laid for Elijah at the Passover seder meal, and Talmudic literature often glosses over unresolved contradictions with the phrase "until Elijah comes." For Christians, Elijah is associated with prophecies concerning the coming of the Messiah.

Unlike Isaiah, Ezekiel, and company, Elijah—here pictured in a fresco from an Orthodox monastery in Serbia—left us no book of writings bearing his name, yet he is revered as perhaps the greatest Old Testament prophet. When Jesus was transfigured on a mountaintop (see pages 132–133), Elijah appeared alongside him as a representative of all the prophets, together with Moses, representing the Jewish Law.

ELIJAH TAKEN UP TO HEAVEN

the 30-second bible

Elijah—an Israelite prophet of the ninth century BCE—is talking with his disciple, Elisha, about his imminent departure when suddenly a fiery chariot and horses comes between them and Elijah is taken up to heaven in a whirlwind. Other Israelite prophets recognize that Elijah's spirit now rests upon Elisha—precisely what Elisha had asked for as a last bequest from his master. The dramatic end to his ministry helped to make Elijah a focus of subsequent prophecy. Malachi declared that the prophet would come to restore Israel to piety and thus avert God's terrible judgment. Centuries later, the angel Gabriel alluded to this prophecy, when he announced that John the Baptist would operate in Elijah's spirit. Many Jews anticipated Elijah's return as the forerunner of the Messiah, yet when John the Baptist appeared in the wilderness, calling for repentance and pointing to the one—namely Jesus—who would bring salvation by removing the world's sins, Jesus castigated them for failing to equate him with Elijah. When Jesus was later transfigured, Moses and Elijah appeared alongside him, their presence indicating that both the Law and the Prophets, which respectively they represent, bear witness to Jesus as the Messiah.

3-SECOND SERMON
The prominent prophet Elijah is taken up to heaven in a whirlwind, his name subsequently becoming associated with messianic prophecy.

3-MINUTE MEDITATION
When confronted by fellow Jews, John the Baptist (see pages 126–127) denied being the actual Elijah. He functioned, however, in Elijah's spirit, as Gabriel had announced he would. Did John's ministry fulfill Elijah's mission? Some think the prophet still has a role to fulfill, since Malachi's prophecy places Elijah before Judgment Day: a day of terror to some, yet of salvation to those who heed his call.

CHAPTER & VERSE
See
2 KINGS 2.1–18

RELATED STORIES
See also
THE TRANSFIGURATION
page 132
MALACHI 4.5–6
MATTHEW 11.14, 17.10–13
LUKE 1.11–17
JOHN 1.19–21

KEY QUOTE
As they continued walking and talking, a chariot of fire and horses of fire separated the two of them, and Elijah ascended in a whirlwind into heaven.
2 KINGS 2.11

30-SECOND TEXT
Stefan Bosman

Elijah is one of just two biblical figures said to have been taken up into heaven instead of having died. The other was Enoch—an early descendant of Adam.

WORDS OF WISDOM

Babylonian exile The deportation of Jews to Babylon in 598, 587, and 582 BCE, following the fall of Judah to the Babylonians. Their exile came to an end in 538 BCE, when the conquering Persian king, Cyrus the Great, gave them permission to return to Jerusalem and rebuild the Temple there.

Canaanites Inhabitants from about 3000–1000 BCE of the region between the Jordan River and the Mediterranean, claimed by the Israelites as the Promised Land.

ecumenical Of worldwide scope and significance; in relation to the Christian Church, concerned with the establishing and promotion of unity between various branches and denominations.

mystical writings The writings of those seeking through contemplation and submission to become one with the divine.

Passover A seven- or eight-day Jewish spring festival that celebrates the deliverance of the Israelites from their time of slavery in Egypt.

St. John of the Cross (1542–1591) Born near Ávila, in Spain, he was a poet, scholar, and mystic, and cofounder of the monastic order known as the Discalced Carmelites.

The Psalms
Some interesting facts about the Psalms:
- There are 150 psalms in all, comprising 2,461 verses.
- Psalm 117, at just two verses, is the shortest; Psalm 119, with 176, the longest.
- Probably the best-known psalm is Psalm 23: "The Lord is my shepherd."
- Almost half (seventy-three) of the Psalms are attributed to David, twelve to Asaph (Psalms 50, 73–83), eleven to the Korahites (Psalms 42, 44–49, 84–85, 87–88), two to Solomon (Psalms 72 and 127), one to Moses (Psalm 90), one to Heman the Ezrahite (Psalm 88), and one to Ethan the Ezrahite (Psalm 89). There are fifty that are anonymous.
- The Psalms are quoted or alluded to in the New Testament more frequently than any other Old Testament book—about a hundred times in all.
- Some of the Psalms are arranged acrostically, the first word of verses or part verses beginning, in sequence, with one of the twenty-two letters of the Hebrew alphabet. Psalms 9, 10, and 37 start with a new letter every two verses, Psalms 25, 34, and 145 every one, Psalms 111 and 112 every half a verse, and Psalm 119 every eight.

Prophets

There are fifteen books attributed to prophets in the Old Testament, roughly dated as follows:

The Major Prophets

Isaiah (740–687 BCE[1])
Jeremiah (626–605 BCE)
Ezekiel (593–571 BCE)

The Minor Prophets

Hosea (783–732 BCE)
Joel (ca. 400 BCE)
Amos (783–743 BCE)
Obadiah (848–841 BCE)
Jonah (782–753 BCE)
Micah (735–700 BCE)
Nahum (614 BCE)
Habakkuk (605–597 BCE)
Zephaniah (640–609 BCE)
Haggai (520 BCE)
Zechariah (519–480 BCE)
Malachi (450 BCE)

The Books of the Apocrypha

The following apocryphal books were published in the 1611 King James Bible:

1 Esdras (ca. 150 BCE)
2 Esdras (ca. 100 CE)
Tobit (ca. 200 BCE)
Judith (ca. 150 CE)
Additions to Esther (ca. 130 BCE)
Wisdom of Solomon (30 BCE)
Ecclesiasticus (32 BCE)
Baruch (ca. 100 CE)
Letter of Jeremiah (ca. 200 BCE)
Prayer of Azariah (ca. 100 BCE)
Susanna (Daniel 13); (ca. 100 BCE)
Bel and the Dragon (ca. 100 BCE)
Prayer of Manasseh (ca. 150 BCE)
1 Maccabees (ca. 110 BCE)
2 Maccabees (ca. 100 BCE)

[1] Many scholars distinguish Isaiah 40–55 and 56–66 from chapters 1–39, ascribing these to later authors, writing under Isaiah's name.

THE TRIALS OF JOB

the 30-second bible

3-SECOND SERMON
God permits Satan to afflict His righteous servant Job to prove that Job will not curse God's name.

3-MINUTE MEDITATION
The story emphasizes that God's power over creation is absolute, and that only God can judge what is good and what is evil. Job's friends argue that evil is the result of sin, and conversely that prosperity is a divine gift to the righteous. The story challenges this simplistic understanding of evil, and reminds readers that God's ways are ultimately mysterious.

The book of Job is a thought-provoking meditation on the origins and meaning of suffering. Job is a prosperous and pious landowner, whose faithfulness God commends to Satan (meaning "adversary" or "prosecutor"), one of the heavenly beings. Satan avers that Job praises God only because he is prosperous, and that he would curse God if his prosperity were taken away. God, therefore, permits Satan to afflict Job with the death of his children, the decimation of his flocks, and a scourge upon his bodily health. His wife urges Job to curse God, but Job remains firm in faith. Job's friends, reflecting the conventional wisdom, try to persuade him that he must have committed some sin to incur divine wrath, but Job maintains his innocence. Finally, he demands that God answer for what has happened. God reprimands Job, saying that only He, the Lord, constructed the world and everything in it, and that only He can understand the reasons why good and evil happen. Job repents of his demand to know the Lord's ways, and humbles himself in dust and ashes. In an epilogue, possibly written later, God restores to Job twice what he had before his affliction.

CHAPTER & VERSE
See
JOB 1.1–42.17

RELATED STORIES
See also
SATAN
pages 22–23
MARK 1.12–13

KEY QUOTE
Have pity on me, have pity on me, O you my friends, for the hand of God has touched me!
JOB 19.21

30-SECOND TEXT
Tim Muldoon

Is suffering God's punishment for sin? Not according to the book of Job, which was written precisely to counter such a simplistic assumption.

PSALMS

the 30-second bible

The Greek word *psalmos* means "a text set to music"; "Praise him with trumpet sound," says Psalm 150.3; "praise him with lute and harp!" These 150 songs of varying length were at some point in biblical history attributed to King David, several quite explicitly (for example, Psalm 51; see page 66). They were composed over as many as five centuries and reflect varying styles, moods, even theologies. Presumed to be among the oldest, Psalm 29, reflects ancient Canaanite belief in multiple gods, whereas other psalms (such as Psalm 137) reflect an awareness of the Babylonian exile in the sixth century BCE. There is no discernible order to the numbering of the Psalms. Rather, they can be organized according to themes, such as lament and praise. The Hebrew name for the book, *tehillim*, "praises," indicates the collection's liturgical use. Even today, monastic communities around the world recite or sing the Psalms multiple times every day, often beginning with the words of Psalm 51.15, "O Lord, open my lips, and my mouth will declare your praise." A common theme through the Psalms is trust in the Lord, exemplified most prominently in the well-known words, "The Lord is my shepherd; there is nothing I shall want" (Psalm 23).

3-SECOND SERMON
The Psalms are among the most ancient and beautiful of biblical texts, written as songs to be performed in the context of worship.

3-MINUTE MEDITATION
The Psalms are the songs of the human heart before God: from suffering, "Out of the depths I cry to you, O Lord. Lord, hear my voice!" (130.1–2a); to thanksgiving, "O give thanks to the Lord, for he is good, for his steadfast love endures forever" (136.1); to simple trust, "The Lord is my shepherd, I shall not want" (23.1); to wonder, "what are human beings that you are mindful of them?" (8.4a).

CHAPTER & VERSE
See
PSALMS 1.1–150.6

RELATED STORIES
See also
DAVID & BATHSHEBA
page 66

KEY QUOTE
Happy are those whose way is blameless, who walk in the law of the Lord. Happy are those who keep his decrees, who seek him with their whole heart, who also do no wrong, but walk in his ways.
PSALM 119.1–3

30-SECOND TEXT
Tim Muldoon

Largely attributed to David—shepherd turned king—the Psalms have been used in worship for nearly three thousand years.

PROVERBS

the 30-second bible

The book of Proverbs reads like instructions from father to son, or from elders to young men preparing to take on public responsibility in ancient Israel. The first nine chapters focus on the pursuit of wisdom, and specifically on the "fear of the Lord" as the beginning of wisdom, particularly in sexual relationships. Three chapters (2, 5, and 7) caution against the "strange woman" (a loose woman or prostitute). By contrast, there are guidelines to choosing a wife (31.10–31), meditations on the virtues of a good wife (5.18–19, 12.4, 18.22, 19.14), and warnings against adultery (5.1–23, 6.20–7.27). The tone of the book is that of conventional wisdom; unlike the prophetic books, in which the prophet speaks for God ("thus says the Lord . . ."), the author of Proverbs wants to pass onto younger men the gathered wisdom of his peers: "Hear, my child, your father's instruction, and do not reject your mother's teaching; for they are a fair garland for your head, and pendants for your neck" (1.8–9). Wisdom is personified as a woman: "Get wisdom; get insight: do not forget, nor turn away from the words of my mouth. Do not forsake her, and she will keep you; love her, and she will guard you" (4.5–6).

3-SECOND SERMON
Attributed to Solomon (1.1, 10.1, 25.1), this collection of sayings focuses on the theme of wisdom leading to prosperity, and foolishness to misery.

3-MINUTE MEDITATION
To this day, the word "proverb" connotes a timeless piece of wisdom, a piece of knowledge forged over many generations. The book of Proverbs presents us with wise sayings collected to guide the people of Israel. Job, however, which is another of the Old Testament's wisdom books, illustrates vividly that wise choices and fear of the Lord do not necessarily guarantee a life of prosperity. God's ways can trump ordinary human wisdom.

CHAPTER & VERSE
See
PROVERBS 1.1–31.31

RELATED STORIES
See also
SOLOMON'S WISDOM
page 68
1 KINGS 4:29–34
THE TRIALS OF JOB
page 78
ECCLESIASTES 1.1–12.13

KEY QUOTE
For the Lord gives wisdom; from his mouth come knowledge and understanding.
PROVERBS 2.6

30-SECOND TEXT
Tim Muldoon

You'll recognize the saying "Pride goes before a fall," but that's just one of many snippets of wisdom to be found in the book of Proverbs—a collection of sayings attributed to King Solomon.

Ο ΠΡΟΦΗΤΗΣ ΗΣΑΪΑΣ

ΕΥΦΡΑΙΝΕ
ΣΘΕ ΟΥΡΑ
ΝΟΙ ΚΑΓΑΛ
ΛΙΑΣΘΩΗ
ΓΗ

ISAIAH

Isaiah was a prophet who lived

in the eighth century BCE, at a time when the Kingdom of Israel had been split into two. Isaiah lived in the southern area—the Kingdom of Judah—centered on Jerusalem. According to the book named after him, the prophet lived through the reigns of four of the kings of Judah: Uzziah (also known as Azariah), Jotham, Ahaz, and Hezekiah. This was a time of great political upheaval and warfare, with Judah's powerful neighbors—the Assyrians and Egyptians—vying for control of the area. In the midst of this, Isaiah prophesies first doom for a sinful nation and then redemption and a new creation in God's Kingdom.

Although the whole book is traditionally ascribed to the historical figure of Isaiah, scholars now agree that the text is an amalgam of writings from three different periods, with only the first section (the first thirty-nine chapters) attributed to Isaiah himself. These chapters include a powerful condemnation of Judah for having lapsed from active faith in God. Instead of putting his trust in God, as Isaiah urges, Ahaz opts instead to trust the temporal protection of the Assyrians. Isaiah's message is consistent throughout his teachings: God's covenant with Israel is a demand for social justice and religious fidelity, not a get-out-of-jail-free card guaranteeing God's blessing.

By contrast, the latter sections of the book of Isaiah look forward to a time when Israel will be delivered from their Babylonian captivity and the land promised to them will be restored. In passages that were later hugely influential for New Testament writers, Isaiah foretells the coming of a "servant of Yahweh," who will establish God's justice across the world, assist those being persecuted, and, strikingly, suffer himself. These "suffering servant" passages are interpreted by Christians as prophesying the coming of Jesus Christ as an innocent who suffers a sacrificial death to bring about God's salvation.

Little is known of Isaiah's life: The text does not even give the name of his wife, who is known only as "the prophetess," and no details are given of his death. It is his powerful visionary writings that have secured his importance within Jewish and Christian traditions. His words continue to inspire humanity's highest aspirations—the famous hymn to peace of Isaiah 2.4, with its image of swords beaten into plowshares, is the unofficial motto of the United Nations.

Listen to Handel's *Messiah* and, although you may not know it, much of the time you'll be listening to the words of Isaiah. The book's influence on New Testament writers and subsequent generations was immense, its prophecies time and again being seen as fulfilled in Jesus. Here, the prophet is pictured in a twentieth-century Greek icon painted in Byzantine style, from Mount Athos, Chalkidike, Greece.

THE SONG OF SOLOMON

the 30-second bible

3-SECOND SERMON
An erotic love poem about
a lover pursuing a beloved,
the Song of Solomon is
seen as an allegory for
the single-minded love
of God for His people.

3-MINUTE MEDITATION
Those who consider
the Bible to be sexually
repressed have not read
the Song of Solomon.
Both Jewish and Christian
commentators stress that
the text extols the more
literal meaning of sexual
love, as well as the
allegorical meaning of
God's passionate and
relentless love for the
souls of the people He
has created. In light
of this text, marriage
has been seen as a
prefiguration of heaven.

This enigmatic text (also called
the Song of Songs or Canticle of Canticles)
contains no mention of God, and yet has been
regarded over the ages as a central allegory for
understanding divine love. It is likely a collection
of ancient love poems, although its sources are
unclear; the text may be rooted in prehistoric
Canaanite worship. The first-century Rabbi
Akiba put it well, suggesting that if the whole
Bible is holy, the Song of Solomon is the "Holy
of Holies," because of the way it describes the
passionate love between the couple, seen to
represent God and Israel. It is read by Jews on
the last day of Passover, and its association
with this spring festival may indicate that the
book is a remnant of an ancient fertility drama.
Its importance in both Jewish and Christian
traditions is primarily allegorical. Christian
writers, such as Bernard of Clairvaux and
John of the Cross, used images from the
book in their mystical writings, suggesting
that sexual love is close to divine love.
What is remarkable in the text is that both
protagonists—man and woman—desire the
other passionately. In particular, the portrayal
of female sexual desire is unique among the
many male-centered biblical texts.

CHAPTER & VERSE
See
SONG OF SOLOMON 1.1–8.14

RELATED STORIES
See also
ISAIAH 54.4–8
JEREMIAH 2.2
HOSEA 1.1–14.9
EPHESIANS 5.23–32
REVELATION 21.2

KEY QUOTE
*Set me as a seal upon your
heart, as a seal upon your arm;
for love is strong as death,
passion fierce as the grave.*
SONG OF SOLOMON 8.6

30-SECOND TEXT
Tim Muldoon

*For all people's
attempts to
spiritualize it, the
Song of Solomon
is essentially a
celebration of human
love and sexuality.*

DANIEL &
THE LIONS' DEN

the 30-second bible

3-SECOND SERMON
Defying an ordinance
against prayer, Daniel is
thrown into a den of lions,
but God preserves him
from harm.

3-MINUTE MEDITATION
The book of Daniel is part
of the genre known as
apocalyptic, a type of
literature that appeals to
an oppressed people and
that emphasizes God's
ultimate power over
creation. The story of
Daniel and the lions' den
can be read as a parable of
this divine power: all may
appear lost, it suggests to
us, but ultimately God is
more powerful than any
law or human ruler.

Under the reign of the Babylonian
king Darius the Mede, the Jewish administrator
Daniel has distinguished himself among his
peers, who, consumed by jealousy, seek to
destroy him. Knowing that Daniel unfailingly
prays three times a day in his rooms, they
appeal to King Darius to publish an ordinance
prohibiting any form of prayer, except to
Darius himself, for thirty days, under penalty of
being thrown into a den of lions. Their trap is
successful and they catch Daniel praying, which
they duly report to Darius. The king is dismayed
but cannot dispute that Daniel is clearly guilty
under the new ordinance, so when pressed to
levy the punishment, he has no choice but to
agree. He stays awake and fasts throughout
the night, however, hoping that Daniel might
somehow survive. At daybreak, he hurries to
the den and calls for Daniel, who responds
that the Lord has preserved him, an upright
man loyal to the king. Delighted and relieved,
Darius frees Daniel and, in his place, throws
his accusers and their families to the lions,
which immediately overpower them. The
story concludes with Darius decreeing that
people throughout the "whole world" should
fear Daniel's God. For Jews and Christians alike,
Daniel is a shining example of courage and
faithfulness in the face of persecution.

CHAPTER & VERSE
See
DANIEL 6.1–28

RELATED STORIES
See also
BEL AND THE DRAGON
(from the Apocrypha)
page 77

KEY QUOTE
*My God sent his angel and shut
the lions' mouths so that they
would not hurt me, because
I was found blameless before
him; and also before you,
O king, I have done no wrong.*
DANIEL 6.22

30-SECOND TEXT
Tim Muldoon

*The Bible may be a
closed book for many,
but the story of Daniel
in the lions' den is one
of those classic tales
everyone seems to
have heard of.*

JONAH &
THE WHALE

the 30-second bible

In the eighth century BCE, God commissions Jonah, an Israelite, to proclaim to the city of Nineveh that it would be destroyed for its wickedness. However, Jonah flees from his assignment by taking a ship in the opposite direction. A storm erupts and Jonah, knowing he is its cause, tells the sailors to throw him overboard. Reluctantly they comply. The storm abates and they worship Jonah's God. A big fish—traditionally identified as a whale, although the text is not specific—swallows Jonah. After being inside it for three days, Jonah repents and is spat out ashore. Arriving in Nineveh, Jonah delivers his message, whereupon the king decrees that everyone should turn from their evil ways. When God consequently decides not to destroy Nineveh, Jonah—who believes its citizens should be punished rather than forgiven—sulks furiously outside the city. His rage is increased when a bush that God provides for shade withers and dies. God, however, points out that if Jonah is right to be upset about a mere plant, then surely the fate of numerous people, ignorant of right and wrong, matters far more. This object lesson summarizes three main themes. First, God does not hold one accountable for what one does not know. Second, God cares about everyone, not just Israelites. Third, God mercifully responds to repentance.

3-SECOND SERMON
God lets a disobedient fugitive prophet, Jonah, be swallowed by a large fish, inside which Jonah comes to his senses, and he subsequently fulfills his commission.

3-MINUTE MEDITATION
Against the background of Jonah's attempt to flee his prophetic commission stands the animosity between the Israelites and Ninevites (Assyrians). Ironically, the Israelite prophet is initially disobedient and takes three days to repent, while the gentile Ninevites wholeheartedly turn from evil. Jesus alluded to this contrast when his unreceptive Jewish audience demanded a sign. He said that they would receive no sign other than that of Jonah (Matthew 16.4; Luke 11.29–30).

CHAPTER & VERSE
See
JONAH 1.1–4.11

RELATED STORIES
See also
2 KINGS 14.25
MATTHEW 12.38–41
LUKE 11.29–32

KEY QUOTE
And should I not be concerned about Nineveh, that great city, in which there are more than a hundred and twenty thousand people who do not know their right hand from their left, and also many animals?
JONAH 4.11

30-SECOND TEXT
Stefan Bosman

Most people know that Jonah was swallowed by a whale, but do they know that it was God's way of calling a reluctant prophet back to duty?

THE APOCRYPHA

the 30-second bible

The term "apocrypha" means "hidden" in Greek, and may refer to the fact that some reformers wanted these books removed from the Catholic and Orthodox canons of the Bible. A "canon" (Greek for "measure") is a list of books, and many of the Apocrypha were part of the ancient canon of the Bible translated from Hebrew into Greek in the third and second centuries BCE. The collection includes sixteen texts, some unique, others additions to the biblical books of Daniel, the Psalms, and Esther. The texts range from wisdom literature (Wisdom of Solomon, Sirach—also known as Ecclesiasticus, not to be confused with the book of Ecclesiastes), to poetry (Psalm 151, the Prayer of Azariah, the Prayer of Manasseh), prophecy (the Letter of Jeremiah), "edifying story" (Susanna, Bel and the Dragon, Tobit, Judith), history (1–4 Maccabees, 1–2 Esdras), or a combination of several genres (Baruch). They provide an important glimpse into the Jewish world from the time of the exile in Babylon up to the Maccabean revolt that occurred in the mid-second century BCE, the period immediately preceding the Roman rule of Judea that continued through the time of Jesus. The Apocrypha thus provide important connections between the worlds of the Old and New Testaments.

3-SECOND SERMON
A "second canon" of texts written later than the primary canon of Scripture, this is regarded by some as part of the Bible, but not by others.

3-MINUTE MEDITATION
The history of the Apocrypha raises the ecumenical and interfaith question of how to understand the nature of God's revelation to people over time. Today, in light of increased cooperation among Jewish, Catholic, Orthodox, and Protestant biblical scholars, there is more understanding of this question. Rather than seeing biblical revelation as a single unmediated utterance of God, scholars typically understand revelation as a process involving composition, reception, and enactment of a community's understanding of God over history.

CHAPTER & VERSE
See
THE BOOKS OF
THE APOCRYPHA
page 77

RELATED STORIES
See also
JUDGES 1.1–21.25
2 CHRONICLES 33.1–25
SONG OF SOLOMON
page 86
JEREMIAH 1.1–52.34

KEY QUOTE
Great is truth, and strongest of all!
1 ESDRAS 4.41

30-SECOND TEXT
Tim Muldoon

Helping to bridge the gap between the writing of the Old Testament and that of the New, the Apocrypha's status as Scripture continues to be debated.

A NEW TESTAMENT

angel Although angels are typically depicted in art with wings and a halo, the term angel (Hebrew *mal'akh*; Greek *angelos*) in the Bible means simply a messenger sent by God, usually but not always from heaven.

Eucharistic Related to Holy Communion, otherwise known as Mass or the Lord's Supper, through which Christians remember and celebrate the Last Supper that Jesus shared with his apostles (see pages 110–111)

Gabriel The angel Gabriel, whose name means "God is my strength," is mentioned twice in the Bible. In the Old Testament, he appears to Daniel and reveals the meaning of Nebuchadnezzar's dreams. In the New, he announces to Mary that she is to give birth to the promised Son of God. According to Muslim tradition, Gabriel dictated the Qur'an to Muhammad.

Jeremiah An Old Testament prophet whose ministry spanned the years leading up to and including the time of the Judeans' exile in Babylon (597 BCE).

"suffering servant" songs Passages in the book of Isaiah that speak of a servant of God who will suffer to redeem His people.

Jesus' Genealogy
The Gospels of Matthew and Luke both trace the genealogy of Jesus. The shortest list (Matthew 1.1–17) places him in the line of the Judean royal family:

↓ Abraham
↓ Isaac
↓ Jacob
↓ Judah (husband of Tamar)
↓ Perez
↓ Hezron
↓ Ram
↓ Amminadab
↓ Nahshon
↓ Salmon (husband of Rahab)
↓ Boaz (husband of Ruth)
↓ Obed
↓ Jesse
↓ David (king of Israel)
↓ Solomon (son of David and Bathsheba)
↓ Rehoboam (king of Israel, later of Judah)
↓ Abijam (king of Judah)
↓ Asa (king of Judah)
↓ Jehosaphat (king of Judah)
↓ Jehoram (king of Judah)
↓ Uzziah (king of Judah)
↓ Jotham (king of Judah)
↓ Ahaz (king of Judah)
↓ Hezekiah (king of Judah)
↓ Manasseh (king of Judah)
↓ Amon (king of Judah)

↓ Josiah (king of Judah)
↓ Jeconiah (king of Judah in exile)
↓ Shealtiel (king of Judah in exile)
↓ Zerubbabel (grandson of Jeconiah and governor of Judah)
↓ Abiud
↓ Eliakim
↓ Azor
↓ Zadok
↓ Achim
↓ Eliud
↓ Eleazar
↓ Matthan
↓ Jacob
↓ Joseph (husband of Mary)
↓ Jesus

The Beatitudes

The blessings promised by Jesus in his Sermon on the Mount (Matthew 5) are as follows:

- Blessed are the poor in spirit, for theirs is the kingdom of heaven (v. 3).
- Blessed are those who mourn, for they will be comforted (v. 4).
- Blessed are the meek, for they will inherit the earth (v. 5).
- Blessed are those who hunger and thirst for righteousness, for they will be filled (v. 6).
- Blessed are the merciful, for they will receive mercy (v. 7).
- Blessed are the pure in heart, for they will see God (v. 8).
- Blessed are the peacemakers, for they will be called children of God (v. 9).
- Blessed are those who are persecuted for righteousness' sake, for theirs is the kingdom of heaven (v. 10).

The Apostles

The twelve apostles of Jesus were:

Simon Peter (originally named Simon, Jesus renamed him Peter, meaning "the rock")
Andrew (brother of Simon Peter): Also a fisherman from Bethsaida
James (son of Zebedee, brother of John)
John (son of Zebedee, brother of James)
Philip
Bartholomew (identified with the Nathanael mentioned in John 1.45–51)
Thomas (remembered for doubting the Resurrection)
Matthew (the tax collector)
James (son of Alphaeus)
Thaddaeus (also known as Judas or Jude)
Simon (the Zealot)
Judas Iscariot (who betrayed Jesus)

After Judas hanged himself, following his betrayal of Jesus, he was replaced by Matthias. Paul also described himself as an apostle.

THE ANNUNCIATION

the 30-second bible

The angel Gabriel appears to

Mary, a young Jewish girl betrothed to a man named Joseph. The angel announces that she will bear "the Son of the Most High." To her amazement, the angel explains: "The Holy Spirit will . . . overshadow you . . . [and] the child . . . will be holy . . . the Son of God.". Mary responds with unflinching faith: "Here am I, the servant of the Lord; let it be to me according to your word." The language of "overshadowing" here is reminiscent of God's presence "filling" the Tabernacle (Exodus 40.35), where the Greek Old Testament uses the same Greek word, *episkiazo*. Also, the phrase "the Lord is with you," used here by the angel with reference to Mary, occurs throughout the Bible in order to indicate God's presence and support for accomplishing His mission, as, for example, with Moses (Exodus 3.12), Joshua (Joshua 1.5, 9), and Gideon (Judges 6.12). This means that Mary, too, stands on the cusp of some great moment in salvation history; and indeed, her "yes" to the angel makes way for the grand climax of the entire Bible—the Cross and Resurrection of Jesus Christ. God is free to save how He sees fit, but here His plan hangs on the faith and obedience of the Virgin Mary; and for that, she is called "blessed" (Luke 1.42).

3-SECOND SERMON
The angel Gabriel appears to Mary and announces that she will become the virgin mother of the Son of God.

3-MINUTE MEDITATION
This child, Mary is told, will be given the "throne of his ancestor David." Behind these words stand God's promises to David of an everlasting kingdom, a kingdom that, historically, was decimated by the Babylonians in the sixth century BCE. The angel's message touches upon this hope of Israel: Jesus will restore the Davidic Kingdom and bring to fulfillment the long-awaited promises to David.

CHAPTER & VERSE
See
LUKE 1.26–56

RELATED STORIES
See also
2 SAMUEL 7.12–17
LUKE 1.57–80

KEY QUOTE
The angel said to her, "Do not be afraid, Mary, for you have found favor with God. And now, you will conceive in your womb and bear a son, and you will name him Jesus."
LUKE 1.30–31

30-SECOND TEXT
Andrew D. Swafford

You will bear a son, Gabriel tells Mary—a child who will change not only her life but the world itself, for he will be called "Son of God."

THE NATIVITY

the 30-second bible

3-SECOND SERMON
Matthew and Luke tell the
story of Jesus' birth as a
unique event in Israelite
and world history.

3-MINUTE MEDITATION
Whereas Matthew begins
with a genealogy that
shows Jesus' relationship
to key Old Testament
figures, such as Abraham
and King David, Luke
begins his story with the
birth of John the Baptist
(see pages 126–127) and
the Annunciation (see
pages 98–99). After his
birth, Jesus is taken by
Mary and Joseph to the
Temple, where, Luke tells
us, an elder named Simeon
praises God in a beautiful
prayer known today as
the *Nunc Dimittis* (Luke
2.29–32). The prophetess
Anna similarly gives
thanks to God.

Of the four Gospels, only two
have stories about the birth of Jesus. Matthew's
story emphasizes that a new king has been
born, in fulfillment of Old Testament prophecies,
whereas Luke stresses that Jesus has come to
serve the poor. In Matthew, an angel tells
Joseph in a dream to wed Mary, although she is
already mysteriously pregnant. The angel quotes
lines from the prophet Isaiah about the coming
of Emmanuel ("God is with us"), which originally
referred to King Cyrus of Persia liberating Israel
from exile in Babylon. Joseph obeys, and names
Mary's child Jesus. Wise men from the East
later follow a star and come to pay homage to
the child, symbolizing that he is to be king not
just of Israel but over all nations. Luke tells us
more about the actual birth of Jesus. When
Augustus Caesar orders a census throughout
the empire, the heavily pregnant Mary travels
with Joseph to her husband's birthplace of
Bethlehem, where—unable to find a room for
the night in the crowded inns—she gives birth
to Jesus in a stable. Angels appear to shepherds
in the fields and announce the birth of a
savior—"good news of great joy for all the
people" (Luke 2.10)—upon which the shepherds
hurry to adore the infant, returning home
glorifying and praising God.

CHAPTER & VERSE
See
MATTHEW 1.1–2.23
LUKE 1.1–2.38

RELATED STORIES
See also
ISAIAH
page 84
THE ANNUNCIATION
page 98

KEY QUOTE
*. . . to you is born this day in the
city of David a Savior, who is
the Messiah, the Lord.*
LUKE 2.11

30-SECOND TEXT
Tim Muldoon

*Shepherds and wise
men kneeling in
wonder before the
Christ-child as Mary
and Joseph gaze
adoringly into the
manger—the classic
nativity scene.*

MARY

Mary, the mother of Jesus, is one of the most important women in the Bible, yet there are surprisingly few specific references to her in the New Testament writings. The most detail is given in the context of the Nativity (see pages 100–101), but Mary is also present with Jesus at several key moments in his life—and afterward.

Identified in Luke's Gospel as a cousin of Elizabeth, wife of the priest Zechariah, Mary is described as a virgin (*parthenos*) betrothed to Joseph when she is visited by the angel Gabriel (see pages 98–99). No details of her age are given, but she was probably 12–13 years old when she became miraculously pregnant with Jesus. Luke tells of Mary receiving the shepherds and wise men, and of her giving offerings in the Temple after Jesus' birth, before returning to Nazareth. One particularly poignant detail is Mary's response to the praise lavished upon Jesus by the shepherds— "Mary treasured all these words and pondered them in her heart" (Luke 2.19).

Mary also features in the one event of Jesus' childhood related in the Gospels, anxiously searching for her 12-year-old son after he becomes separated from Joseph and herself during the Passover festivities in Jerusalem. They find him in the Temple, precociously conversing with the priests.

John's Gospel reports that it is Mary who prompts Jesus to perform his first miracle of turning water into wine at a wedding feast in Cana (see pages 122–123). It also places her at the Crucifixion, where Jesus entrusts her into the care of the intriguing figure known as the "beloved disciple."

Finally, Mary is listed in Acts as present with the eleven apostles in the upper room after Jesus' Ascension. This is the last explicit mention of Mary in the Bible, which contains no reference to her death, nor to the traditional Christian teaching that she was taken bodily (assumed) into heaven.

Apocryphal and subsequent writings abound with further details of Mary's life, filling in the gaps in the Gospel narrative and illustrating points of theology. A good example is the doctrine of the "Immaculate Conception," according to which Mary was conceived by her parents, Joachim and Anne (not named in the Bible), without the stain of original sin.

Although she features only briefly in the Bible, Mary is celebrated within the Church as a paradigm of faith for her openness and obedience to God's will. Typically portrayed holding the infant Jesus in her arms—the classic Madonna and child image, shown here in stained glass—she was to experience heartbreak as well as joy, watching helplessly as her son suffered and died on the Cross.

JESUS' BAPTISM IN THE JORDAN

the 30-second bible

Jesus approaches John the

Baptist in the wilderness and, despite John's reservations, insists upon being baptized. One may wonder why baptism—a symbol of repentance and new beginnings—is appropriate for Jesus, but the reason lies in the internal logic of Christianity itself: God comes to meet man in the very depths of the human condition. Thus, Jesus enters the waters of the Jordan to enter completely into humanity's plight. This sets the stage for the uniqueness of his mission, which is reinforced when he comes up out of the water and hears a voice saying: "This is my Son . . . with whom I am well pleased"—a combination of words from a well-known royal Davidic Psalm (2.7) and the first of the "suffering servant" songs in Isaiah (42.1). This juxtaposition suggests that Jesus will be a different kind of king, one who conquers by way of his own self-offering, not through military might. The life of Christian discipleship, then, consists in continuing this outpouring of Jesus' life in and through one's own life, emulating the master as perfectly as possible; this is accomplished by the power of the Spirit, the fruit of Jesus' mission, which begins here in his baptism and culminates on the Cross.

3-SECOND SERMON
Jesus receives God's seal of approval after being baptized by John the Baptist in the Jordan River.

3-MINUTE MEDITATION
Crossing the Jordan River marked the culmination of the first Exodus and the entrance of the Israelites into the Promised Land. Jesus' baptism in the Jordan, then, evokes a hope for a new exodus, a new deliverance—not so much from without, but from within: a deliverance from sin and death. In this sense, Jesus' mission begins by tapping into the historical hope of Israel, while simultaneously transcending it with heavenly and spiritual dimensions.

CHAPTER & VERSE
See
MATTHEW 3.13–17
MARK 1.9–11
LUKE 3.21–22

RELATED STORIES
See also
JOSHUA 4.1–24
PSALM 2.7
ISAIAH 42.1, 52.13–53.12

KEY QUOTE
*And a voice from heaven said,
"This is my Son, the Beloved,
with whom I am well pleased."*
MATTHEW 3.17

30-SECOND TEXT
Andrew D. Swafford

"I am not worthy to carry his sandals," says John (Matthew 3.11), yet Jesus comes to him by the Jordan River, and asks for baptism.

THE SERMON ON THE MOUNT

the 30-second bible

3-SECOND SERMON
Jesus preaches to a crowd about the Kingdom of God, using a number of vivid images to call people to love as God does.

3-MINUTE MEDITATION
The most paradoxical of Jesus' teachings in the sermon are about love, especially of enemies. Both Matthew and Luke describe love as a perfection of the kind of life that manifests the Kingdom of God, in contrast to the tendency toward self-centeredness among the materially well off. What makes the poor, sorrowful, and humble of the earth inherit the Kingdom of God, he suggests, is their ability to let go of inordinate self-love for the sake of others.

Matthew places this sermon, which features some of the best-known sayings and teaching of Jesus, on a mountainside, where a large crowd had gathered to listen to this fascinating itinerant preacher and healer. The sermon begins with the Beatitudes (from the Latin *beatus*, meaning "happy" or "blessed"), a list of the kinds of people who receive God's blessing. Challenging conventional wisdom, Jesus suggests that this belongs especially to the poor, hungry, sorrowful, and reviled of the earth. In Luke's abbreviated version of the sermon, which is set on "a level place" rather than mountain, Jesus goes on from the Beatitudes to critique those who are considered rich and successful, indicating that eternal rather than temporal concerns are what matter. Both versions of the sermon—of which snippets can also be found in Mark's Gospel—present a short course on following Jesus. Matthew, writing primarily for a Jewish audience, focuses on Jesus' teachings as the perfection of Jewish laws (for example, on anger, marriage, and oaths), and includes the Lord's Prayer (6.9–13), as well as teachings about fasting, money, and authentic discipleship. Luke, who wrote for non-Jews, instead emphasizes love of enemies as the cornerstone of the good life.

CHAPTER & VERSE
See
MATTHEW 5.1–7.28
LUKE 6.17–49

RELATED STORIES
See also
MARK 1.21–22, 4.21, 4.24–25, 9.43–50, 11.25

KEY QUOTE
Blessed are the poor in spirit, for theirs is the kingdom of heaven.
MATTHEW 5.3

30-SECOND TEXT
Tim Muldoon

Love your enemies, turn the other cheek, and do as you would be done by—just some of the timeless teachings of Jesus from the Sermon on the Mount.

JESUS' ENTRY INTO JERUSALEM

the 30-second bible

Jesus has kept his Messianic

identity quiet (Matthew 16.20), but now he enters Jerusalem on a donkey—and the crowd readily understands what this means, shouting, "Hosanna to the Son of David!" and "Blessed is the king who comes in the name of the Lord." Jesus' actions draw from a prophecy found in Zechariah: "Rejoice greatly, O daughter Zion! Shout aloud, O daughter Jerusalem! Lo, your king comes to you; triumphant and victorious is he, humble and riding on a donkey, on a colt, the foal of a donkey." Here, Jesus stands in a long line of prophets who prophesied not just with their words, but also with their *actions*— as, for example, when Jeremiah smashed a jar in Jerusalem to symbolize coming judgment (Jeremiah 19.10). Jesus, here, deliberately evokes the prophecy from Zechariah, proclaiming himself as Messiah—and the crowd recognizes him as such, spreading branches along the road to welcome him. But Christ's kingship is unique, for his victory is won not by the blade of a sword, but by his blood poured out on the Cross. Liturgically, Jesus' entry into Jerusalem is celebrated on Palm Sunday, when Christians welcome him as their king, as he moves toward his singular victory over sin and death, which is celebrated the following week on Good Friday (Crucifixion) and Easter Sunday (Resurrection).

3-SECOND SERMON
Jesus enters Jerusalem on a donkey and is welcomed by branch-waving crowds as their long-awaited Davidic king.

3-MINUTE MEDITATION
After his entry into Jerusalem, Jesus enters the Temple overturning the money-changers' tables; he then cites two Old Testament passages (Isaiah 56.7; Jeremiah 7.11), which explain the meaning of his actions. The first emphasizes God's plan for *all nations*; however, in Jesus' day, the Temple had become a great symbol of Jewish *separation*. Jesus' actions, then, condemn this nationalistic attitude and prophetically foretell the Temple's impending destruction.

CHAPTER & VERSE
See
MATTHEW 21.1–11
MARK 11.1–11
LUKE 19.28–40

RELATED STORIES
See also
ZECHARIAH 9.9–10
MATTHEW 21.12–13

KEY QUOTE
The crowds that went ahead of him and that followed were shouting, "Hosanna to the Son of David! Blessed is the one who comes in the name of the Lord! Hosanna in the highest heaven!"
MATTHEW 21.9

30-SECOND TEXT
Andrew D. Swafford

Cheering crowds welcome Jesus into Jerusalem as their king, but his crown is to be one of thorns and his kingdom won through a cross.

THE LAST SUPPER

the 30-second bible

3-SECOND SERMON
Celebrating the Passover with the apostles, Jesus bids his final farewell, fulfilling by his death and Resurrection the long-awaited hope of Israel.

3-MINUTE MEDITATION
The original context of the Last Supper is the Jewish feast of Passover, which celebrates Israel's deliverance from Egypt, the central feature of which was the slaying and consuming of a lamb. But, surprisingly, the Last Supper nowhere even mentions a lamb. The reason: Jesus is the new Passover Lamb, and his work inaugurates a new exodus—but this time not from Egypt or some political power, but from sin and death.

The night before Jesus died, he gathered the apostles for a Passover meal, during which he referred to bread and wine as his "body" and "blood." "This is my blood of the covenant," he said, "poured out . . . for the forgiveness of sins" (Matthew 26.28). The phrase, the "blood of the covenant," draws from Exodus 24.8, where Moses first ratified the covenant through sacrifice, symbolizing a shared life between God and Israel; Jesus' death constitutes the new covenant sacrifice, fulfilling Jeremiah's prophecy of a "new covenant" that would bring about forgiveness of sins (Jeremiah 31.31, 33). In Jesus' day, the Passover evoked great excitement and expectation, recalling God's past deliverance, but also stirring hopes in the present for a new exodus. It is hard to imagine the exhilaration the apostles must have felt: Jesus is announcing the fulfillment of this hope, in and through his blood. The early Christians gathered together, recalling Jesus' mandate that his Eucharistic words be commemorated—"Do this in remembrance of me" (Luke 22.19)—something which quickly became central in the life of the community as a principal way of entering into the very life and death of Christ.

CHAPTER & VERSE
See
MATTHEW 26.17–29
MARK 14.12–25
LUKE 22.7–23
1 CORINTHIANS 11.23–26

RELATED STORIES
See also
EXODUS 12.1–51
JOHN 6.35–59, 19.28–37

KEY QUOTE
This cup that is poured out for you is the new covenant in my blood.
LUKE 22.20

30-SECOND TEXT
Andrew D. Swafford

Across the centuries, Christians have broken bread and shared wine to remember the sacrificial death of Jesus and to anticipate his promised return.

TRIAL & CRUCIFIXION

the 30-second bible

3-SECOND SERMON
The Roman governor of
Jerusalem, Pontius Pilate,
under pressure from the
local religious authorities,
condemns Jesus to death
on a cross.

3-MINUTE MEDITATION
Crucifixion was a
common practice in
imperial Rome. What is
astonishing, however, is
the fact that the Gospel
writers give vivid details
about Jesus' Crucifixion,
which would normally
have been seen as a curse
by God, according to
the author of the Old
Testament book
Deuteronomy (21.22–23;
cf. Galatians 3.13). That
the Cross became the
symbol of Christian faith
is a testimony to how
central this event was
in the consciousness of
the earliest disciples.

The trial and death of Jesus were understood from the beginning as central events in Christian identity, evidenced by the fact that all the Gospels show unusual consistency in their detailed accounts of the story. Jesus is arrested and brought before the Sanhedrin, the Jewish court. Peter, to protect himself, denies knowing Jesus. The Sanhedrin, seeking the death penalty, sends Jesus to Pontius Pilate, the Roman governor, who—despite finding no reason to condemn Jesus and seeking, in vain, to release him—eventually accedes to their wishes in order to placate the mob that the Sanhedrin has stirred up. Pilate hands Jesus over to soldiers, who, after flogging and mocking him, force him to carry a cross to a place known as "The Skull," where they crucify him between two thieves under a sign that reads "the King of the Jews." "Father, forgive them," says Jesus in one version of the story (Luke 23.34); "for they do not know what they are doing." A small group of women—among them, his mother Mary—watch as onlookers continue to taunt Jesus, offering him vinegar to drink as he is dying. "My God, my God, why have you forsaken me?" he cries (Matthew 27.46; Mark 15.34); then, finally, "Father, into your hands I commend my spirit" (Luke 23.46). Moments afterward, he breathes his last.

CHAPTER & VERSE
See
MATTHEW 26.57–27.56
MARK 14.53–15.41
LUKE 22:66–23.49
JOHN 18.19–19.37

RELATED STORIES
See also
JESUS' ENTRY INTO
JERUSALEM
page 108
THE LAST SUPPER
page 110

KEY QUOTE
When they came to the place that is called The Skull, they crucified Jesus there with the criminals, one on his right and one on his left.
LUKE 23.33

30-SECOND TEXT
Tim Muldoon

A reminder of Jesus' suffering and death, the Cross has become the most readily identifiable symbol of the Christian Church.

THE SON OF GOD

gentile Any non-Jewish person and, by extension, anything relating to them.

Messiah A promised deliverer of the Jewish people, foretold in the words of Isaiah and other Old Testament prophets, and expected to preside as king in Jerusalem over a glorious new era for God's people. Christians believe Jesus to be the Messiah, but understand his kingdom to be in heaven rather than on earth.

Pharisees Members of a Jewish movement or party around the time of Jesus who insisted on strict interpretation of the Law of Moses and rigid observance of its cultic rituals. They are associated in the Gospels with a holier-than-thou attitude, contrasted with the humility of repentant "sinners," who recognize their dependence on God's mercy.

salvation In the New Testament, this is understood as deliverance from sin and its attendant punishment, and the receiving of new life that will continue beyond this world into the kingdom of heaven.

Samaritan A person from the district of Samaria, a mountainous region bordering Judah that had once been part of the Northern Kingdom of Israel—the capital of which was called Samaria—before it was overrun by the Assyrians around 720 BCE.

Parables of Jesus
The Gospels contain more than fifty parables told by Jesus, including:
The barren fig tree (Luke 13.6–9)
The good Samaritan (Luke 10.25–37)
The good shepherd (John 10.1–18)
The laborers in the vineyard
    (Matthew 20.1–16)
The landowner and his tenants
    (Matthew 21.33–46; Mark 12.1–12;
    Luke 20.9–18)
The lost coin (Luke 15.8–10)
The lost sheep (Luke 15.4–7)
The mustard seed (Matthew 13.31–32;
    Mark 4.30–32; Luke 13.18–19)
The old and new wine (Matthew 9.17;
    Mark 2.22; Luke 5.37–39)
The pearl of great price (Matthew 13.45–46)
The prodigal son (Luke 15.11–32)
The rich man and Lazarus (Luke 16.19–31)
The rich fool (Luke 12.16–21)
The sheep and goats (Matthew 25.31–46)
The ten talents (Matthew 25.14–30)
The ten virgins (Matthew 25.1–13)
The sower (Matthew 13.3–9, 18–23;
    Mark 4.3–20; Luke 8.4–15)
The vine and its branches (John 15.1–17)

The Miracles of Jesus
Healings
Healing of a blind man at Bethsaida
(Mark 8.22–26)
Healing of a disabled woman (Luke 13.10–17)
Healing of a mute man (Matthew 9.32–33)
Healing of a Canaanite woman's daughter
(Matthew 15.21–28; Mark 7.24–30)
Healing of an epileptic boy (Matthew
17.14–21; Mark 9.17–29; Luke 9.38–43)
Healing of a man born blind (John 9.1–41)
Healing of a man with dropsy (Luke 14.1–4)
Healing of a royal official's son at Capernaum
(John 4.46–54)
Healing of a possessed man in the synagogue
(Mark 1.23–27; Luke 4.33–36)
Healing of a sick man at the pool of
Bethsaida (John 5.1–15)
Healing of Bartimaeus (Matthew 20.29–34[1];
Mark 10.46–52; Luke 18.35–43[2])
Healing of ten lepers (Luke 17.11–19)
Healing of the high priest's servant
(Luke 22.50–51)
Healing of a leper (Matthew 8.1–4;
Mark 1.40–44; Luke 5.12–14)
Healing of a Roman centurion's servant
(Matthew 8.5–13; Luke 7.1–10)
Healing of Peter's mother-in-law
(Matthew 8.14–15; Mark 1.30–31; Luke
4.38–39)
Healing of Legion (Matthew 8.28–34[3];
Mark 5.1–15; Luke 8.27–39)
Healing of a man with palsy (Matthew 9.2–7;
Mark 2.3–12; Luke 5.18–26)

Healing of the woman with an issue of blood
(Matthew 9.20–22; Mark 5.25–34;
Luke 8.43–48)
Healing of two blind men (Matthew 9.27–31)

Raising from the Dead
Raising of a widow's son at Nain (Luke 7.11–17)
Raising of Jairus' daughter (Matthew 9.18–19,
23–26; Mark 5.22–24, 35–43; Luke 8.40–41,
49–56)
Raising of Lazarus (John 11.1–44)

Control over Nature
Stilling of the storm (Matthew 8.23–27;
Mark 4.37–41; Luke 8.22–25)
Feeding of the five thousand (Matthew
14.14–21; Mark 6.30–44; Luke 9.10–17;
John 6.1–14)
Walking on water (Matthew 14.22–32;
Mark 6.47–52; John 6.16–21)
Feeding of the four thousand
(Matthew 15.32–39; Mark 8.1–9)
Withering of a fig tree (Matthew 21.18–22;
Mark 11.12–14, 20–25)
The bumper catch of fish (Luke 5.4–11;
John 21.1–11)
Turning of water into wine (John 2.1–11)

[1] In Matthew, there are two blind men, neither are named.
[2] In Luke, the blind man is not named.
[3] In Matthew, there are two men, neither are named.

THE GOOD SAMARITAN

the 30-second bible

In an incident unique to Luke's Gospel, a lawyer asks Jesus what he must do to inherit eternal life. Jesus responds with the parable of the good Samaritan, a tale of a Jewish traveler from Jerusalem to Jericho who is beaten by robbers and left for dead. A priest and a Levite, anxious to observe religious purity laws, pass him by on the other side of the road, but a Samaritan goes to help him. He cleans the man's wounds, places him on his animal, and takes him to an inn, even paying for the man's keep. To grasp the full force of the parable, we need to understand that, in Jesus' day, Samaritans were despised by Jews, and vice versa—the result of a longstanding feud between them. A Samaritan, then, was the last person Jesus' listeners would have expected to win plaudits, yet the man's simple act of compassion puts to shame those who supposedly understand what God requires. The point is reinforced in Jesus' subsequent exchange with the lawyer. Asked which of the three men proved a neighbor to the man who was robbed, the lawyer singles out the one who offered help. Go and do the same, says Jesus, evincing Luke's concern to show that the way to salvation lies through loving action in the world.

3-SECOND SERMON
A Samaritan shows what it means to be a neighbor by helping a traveler in need.

3-MINUTE MEDITATION
Luke places the parable immediately before the story of Martha and Mary, in which Martha busies herself in the kitchen while Mary listens to Jesus. A story about contemplating Jesus' words, it acts as a kind of counterpoint to that of the good Samaritan, reflecting Luke's dual emphasis on listening to God's word and then acting upon it. After the Martha and Mary story comes the famous "Our Father" prayer, which encapsulates this dual imperative.

CHAPTER & VERSE
See
LUKE 10.25–37

RELATED STORIES
See also
MATTHEW 10.5
LUKE 9.51–56
JOHN 4.7–9

KEY QUOTE
[Jesus asked] "Which of these three, do you think, was a neighbor to the man who fell into the hands of the robbers?" [The lawyer] said, "The one who showed him mercy." Jesus said to him, "Go and do likewise."
LUKE 10.36–37

30-SECOND TEXT
Tim Muldoon

"Who is my neighbor?" asks a lawyer. In his memorable story of the good Samaritan, Jesus turns the question back not just on him, but on everyone.

THE PRODIGAL SON

the 30-second bible

3-SECOND SERMON
A father runs to meet a returning wayward son, caring not for what others might think but only for his son.

3-MINUTE MEDITATION
In context, Jesus is addressing the Pharisees who sought to remain separate from gentiles and sinners, taking pride in their own fidelity. Jesus invites the Pharisees to see themselves in the older brother, while repentant tax-collectors, prostitutes and other such "sinners" are equated with the younger brother. The open-endedness of the parable, then, seems intentional; the Pharisees get to write their own ending: will they rejoice over repentant sinners, or begrudge God's munificent mercy?

This parable features a father and two sons, the younger of whom demands his inheritance. Squandering the money, he eventually finds himself working in gentile territory, ignominiously caring for swine. He finally decides to return home, not expecting to be welcomed back as a son but hoping his father might employ him as a mere hired servant. Catching a glimpse of his son in the distance, the father runs to meet him, hugging and kissing him, before proceeding to clothe him with "a robe—the best one . . . and [to] put a ring on his finger and sandals on his feet." Given that the son had so publicly disgraced the family, the father's actions fly in the face of "respectability." Jesus' message here almost defies belief: that God loves us *this* much, asking only that we take one step toward God, and He will run the rest of the way to meet us; but that is precisely the gospel. The father in the story calls for a celebration, where we finally meet the older brother— incensed at his father's actions. The father attempts to console him, seemingly to no avail; at least that's where the story ends: whether the older brother finally joined the party or persisted in his resentment we never find out.

CHAPTER & VERSE
See
LUKE 15.11–32

RELATED STORIES
See also
2 SAMUEL 12.1–15
LUKE 15.1–10

KEY QUOTE
But we had to celebrate and rejoice, because this brother of yours was dead and has come to life; he was lost and has been found.
LUKE 15.32

30-SECOND TEXT
Andrew D. Swafford

Remorse for our mistakes, God's generous forgiveness, love beyond anything we deserve—key themes of the gospel are covered in this simple yet unforgettable parable.

THE WEDDING AT CANA

the 30-second bible

Mary, Jesus, and some of his disciples were attending a wedding celebration at Cana in Galilee, when the wine ran out. After alerting Jesus to the problem, Mary turned to the servants and directed them: "Do whatever he [Jesus] tells you" (John 2.5). There happened to be six stone jars nearby that were used for Jewish rites of purification (such as hand washing). Jesus directed the servants to fill the jars with water, draw some of the liquid out, and take it to the head steward. To the shock of the servants, the water had become wine, the delicacy of which exceedingly impressed the steward. This narrative is as innocently entertaining as it is dense with meaning. First, the theme of new wine in abundance is a common Old Testament metaphor for the Messianic era. Second, the text tells us that this is the first of Jesus' "signs," which calls to mind the first of Moses' "signs" (the ten plagues), when he turned the Nile water into blood (Exodus 7.14–25). In this deeper sense, then, the wedding at Cana inaugurates the Messianic era in which the old covenant is transformed and fulfilled into the New—a new exodus is dawning, this time from sin and death.

3-SECOND SERMON
Jesus' first public miracle of turning water into wine begins his journey of bringing Israel's story, and that of humanity, to a climax on the Cross.

3-MINUTE MEDITATION
John's Gospel opens with clear allusions to Genesis, using language such as "In the beginning." This Genesis background sheds light on Jesus' reference to Mary as "Woman" (John 2.4): Mary represents the "woman" prophesied in Genesis 3.15—the woman who would one day bear the offspring that would crush the head of the serpent. Jesus' referring to Mary in this way, then, is certainly not an insult but rather signals the breaking in of a new era.

CHAPTER & VERSE
See
JOHN 2.1–11

RELATED STORIES
See also
GENESIS 3.15
ISAIAH 25.6
JOEL 3.18

KEY QUOTE
Everyone serves the good wine first, and then the inferior wine after the guests have become drunk. But you have kept the good wine until now.
JOHN 2.10

30-SECOND TEXT
Andrew D. Swafford

Water into wine; the best wine yet: not just a miracle says John, but a sign—a pointer to who Jesus is and what he comes to do.

LOAVES & FISHES

the 30-second bible

3-SECOND SERMON
Jesus feeds a massive crowd with five loaves and two fish, providing them with more than enough.

3-MINUTE MEDITATION
The story has clear references to the Exodus, when God gave the Israelites manna (bread) in the desert (Exodus 16.1–35). The Evangelists use that idea to suggest a further point: that while Jesus has divine power to feed with bread, what is more important is his ability to give spiritual food. In John, Jesus says "I am the bread of life. Whoever comes to me will never be hungry" (John 6.35).

All four Gospels have substantially similar versions of this story, in which Jesus miraculously produces an abundance of food. The stories underscore Jesus' importance as one who nourishes humanity. Jesus is teaching and healing in a remote place when it gets late in the evening. Concerned that there is nothing to feed the enormous crowd that has gathered around him—five thousand men, plus women and children—the disciples ask Jesus to help. He takes five loaves and two fish—the only food they can muster from among the multitude—and instructs them to distribute these. All eat their fill, and the disciples then gather twelve baskets full of leftovers. Matthew and Mark tell a second, almost identical story shortly afterward in their Gospels (Matthew 16.5–12; Mark 8.14–21), Jesus is this time feeding four thousand men (plus women and children) from seven loaves (and, in Matthew, "a few small fish") with seven baskets of leftover food gathered afterward. Matthew and Mark compare the bread to "the yeast of the Pharisees"—that is, their teaching—whereas John ties it to a discourse about the Bread of Life. The implication is that life is about more than bread, and that what Jesus gives is infinitely more precious.

CHAPTER & VERSE
See
MATTHEW 14.13–21, 15.29–38
MARK 6.32–44, 8.1–9
LUKE 9.10–17
JOHN 6.1–14

RELATED STORIES
See also
EXODUS 16.1–35
MATTHEW 16.5–12
MARK 8.14–21

KEY QUOTE
Taking the five loaves and the two fish, he looked up to heaven, and blessed and broke the loaves, and gave them to his disciples to set before the people; and he divided the two fish among them all.
MARK 6.41–43

30-SECOND TEXT
Tim Muldoon

A few loaves and fishes, not even enough to have fed the apostles, yet in Jesus' hands they nourish a hungry multitude.

JOHN THE BAPTIST

An enigmatic and powerful

presence in the Gospels, John the Baptist is celebrated by Christians as a prophet foretelling the coming of Jesus as the Messiah. In all four Gospels, he is portrayed as preparing the way for Jesus through his call for repentance and practice of baptism.

According to Luke's Gospel, John is the son of the priest Zechariah and Elizabeth, making him a relative of Jesus, although this is not corroborated by the other Gospels. In an account that echoes the birth of the Old Testament prophet Samuel, the angel Gabriel foretells John's birth to an aged Zechariah, who is then struck dumb, only able to speak again when naming his son. Even before he is born, it seems that John recognizes Jesus, leaping in his mother's womb when she is visited by Mary after the Annunciation (see pages 98–99).

The Synoptic Gospels all record John baptizing Jesus in the Jordan River (see pages 104–105) and in John's Gospel, John the Baptist acclaims Jesus as the "Lamb of God" (John 1.29, 35). All four Gospels portray John's mission as fulfilling Old Testament prophecies, in particular Isaiah's promise of a voice crying out in the wilderness to prepare the way of the Lord (Isaiah 40.3; Matthew 3.3; John 1.23). Matthew also tells how John lived in the desert, wearing clothes made of camel hair and eating locusts and wild honey.

The accounts of John's death are placed in the context of Jesus commissioning his disciples to preach and heal in his name, thus further emphasizing John's role as a witness to Jesus. According to Mark's Gospel, John is imprisoned after criticizing King Herod's marriage to his brother's wife, Herodias. The king, however, is afraid of John on account of his righteousness and seeks to protect him, but when he rashly promises to give his wife's daughter—traditionally known as Salome— anything she would like after the girl dances for him at his birthday banquet, Herodias seizes her chance and tells her to ask for John's head on a platter.

Outside of Scripture, the first-century Romano-Jewish historian Josephus refers to John's call for righteous living and purification by baptism, and suggests that the reason for John's death was more political than religious, Herod fearing that John's influence might lead to a rebellion.

John the Baptist's life was entwined with that of Jesus—in some accounts, his second cousin—from the start, Luke placing the stories of their birth side by side. Yet John's was always a supporting role, his mission being to prepare the way of the Lord. Even as crowds flocked to him for baptism, he pointed to the one who would baptize not with water but with the Holy Spirit. He is pictured here in a medieval fresco from Kosovo, Serbia.

HEALING THE SICK
the 30-second bible

The Gospels give numerous

accounts of Jesus' healing miracles. In some instances, Jesus is petitioned to heal, as in Matthew 8.2, where a leper beseeches Jesus to make him clean. On other occasions he is moved to heal without entreaty, such as in Matthew 8.15, where he touches Peter's mother-in-law to heal her fever. Many of those healed are considered unclean and consequently marginalized according to Mosaic Law, for instance, lepers, people of unsound mind deemed "possessed," and a woman suffering constant menstrual bleeding. When a Roman centurion petitions Jesus to heal his paralyzed servant (Matthew 8.5–13; Luke 7.1–10) he is praised—". . . not even in Israel have I found such faith"—after which Jesus heals the servant without even seeing him. Jesus' healings fulfill God's promise in Isaiah to send his anointed servant (Messiah) to save his people: "Then the eyes of the blind shall be opened, and the ears of the deaf unstopped; then the lame shall leap like a deer, and the tongue of the speechless sing for joy" (Isaiah 35.5–6). By his miracles of healing, Jesus demonstrates that he is this anointed one, the long-awaited Messiah.

3-SECOND SERMON
Jesus performs a great many healing miracles, which testify to his power, authority, and compassion in making people whole in body, mind, and spirit.

3-MINUTE MEDITATION
Jesus courts controversy by healing the sick on the Sabbath, which many deem "unlawful." He silences the dissenters with a question, "Is it lawful to do good or to do harm on the Sabbath, to save life or to kill?" (Mark 3.4). Through the healing miracles Jesus not only fulfills the Scriptures about the Messiah and demonstrates his power and compassion, but also shows that he is "above the Law," a factor that leads to his arrest.

CHAPTER & VERSE
See
GLOSSARY & LISTS
pages 116–117

RELATED STORIES
See also
ISAIAH 35.5–6

KEY QUOTE
"Are you the one who is to come, or are we to wait for another?" Jesus answered them, "Go and tell John what you hear and see: the blind receive their sight, the lame walk, the lepers are cleansed, the deaf hear . . ."
MATTHEW 11.3–5

30-SECOND TEXT
Liz Gulliford

Moved by the plight of those broken in body, mind, or spirit, Jesus time and again reached out to make them whole.

THE RAISING OF LAZARUS

the 30-second bible

3-SECOND SERMON
Jesus' act of raising Lazarus from the dead is a climactic "sign," showing his authority in exercising the ultimate power over life and death.

3-MINUTE MEDITATION
The writer of John's Gospel recounts a series of seven miracles—or "signs," as he calls them—through which Christ's glory is demonstrated (2.11) and through which faith is kindled (20.31). The seven are (1) Jesus' turning water into wine, (2) healing an official's son, (3) healing a paralyzed man, (4) feeding a multitude with five loaves and two fishes, (5) walking on water, (6) giving sight to a blind man, and (7) the raising of Lazarus.

In a story unique to John's Gospel, Jesus receives word from two of his friends, Mary and Martha, that their brother Lazarus is ill. Instead of going immediately to his bedside, Jesus decides to wait for two days before making the journey. He sees Lazarus' illness as a means through which God's glory might become manifest. On the way to the house, Jesus tells his disciples plainly that Lazarus has died, a fact confirmed by Martha when she meets Jesus en route to the house. Martha's faith in Jesus' power is absolute: "Lord, if you had been here, my brother would not have died"—a sentiment echoed verbatim by Mary. Despite being told that Lazarus has been dead and entombed in a cave for four days, Jesus orders that the stone sealing the tomb be rolled away. Understandably the mourners protest, but he tells them that those who believe will "see the glory of God." They move the stone to witness a miracle of the highest order: Jesus calls to Lazarus, who emerges alive from the tomb in his grave clothes. While this truly miraculous "sign" leads many to believe in Jesus, it also serves as a catalyst for Jesus' eventual arrest and execution (11:46–53), and anticipates his own triumph over death through his Resurrection.

CHAPTER & VERSE
See
JOHN 11.1–44

RELATED STORIES
See also
MATTHEW 9.18–19, 23–25
MARK 5.22–24, 35–43
LUKE 7.11–17
LUKE 8.40–42, 49–56

KEY QUOTE
I am the resurrection and the life. Those who believe in me, even though they die, will live, and everyone who lives and believes in me will never die.
JOHN 11.25–26

30-SECOND TEXT
Liz Gulliford

Famously, on finding that his friend Lazarus had died and been sealed in a tomb, Jesus wept, but the story ends not with death but with Resurrection.

THE TRANSFIGURATION

the 30-second bible

3-SECOND SERMON
Peter, James, and John
accompany Jesus up a
mountain, where they
see him transformed,
becoming dazzlingly
bright, in the company
of Elijah and Moses.

3-MINUTE MEDITATION
In some Gospel stories,
Jesus quiets those who
want to proclaim him to
be the Messiah (Mark
1.43–45, 8.29–30), as
if to suggest that God
wants to attract people
not through shows of
divine power, but through
signs of compassion,
such as healing and the
forgiveness of sins. In this
story, however, Peter,
James, and John, having
already fully committed
their lives to Jesus, are
privileged to glimpse
the full manifestation
of his glory.

The story of the Transfiguration is a short but vivid account of a remarkable experience shared by three of Jesus' closest followers: Peter, James, and John. Jesus leads the three disciples up a mountain, where, we read, "his face shone like the sun, and his clothes became dazzling white" (Matthew 17.2). Suddenly, Moses (see pages 48–49) and Elijah (see pages 70–71)—two key figures of Jewish history—appear alongside Jesus, engaging him in conversation. Dumbstruck, Peter offers to build three tabernacles (literally "tents") to mark the occasion, but he is interrupted by a voice from heaven proclaiming, "This is my Son, the Beloved . . . listen to him!" (Matthew 17.5; Mark 9.7). The three disciples are completely overwhelmed by what they have witnessed and at a loss to understand it. The significance of the event seems to be threefold. First, the presence of Moses and Elijah indicates that both the Law and the Prophets, which respectively they represent, bear witness to Jesus as the Messiah. Second, Jesus' radiant appearance and the voice acclaiming him from heaven bear witness to his intimate relationship with the Father. Third, it is an important foreshadowing of the glory that Jesus will achieve by his rising from the dead.

CHAPTER & VERSE
See
MATTHEW 17.1–9
MARK 9.2–10
LUKE 9.28–36

RELATED STORIES
See also
MATTHEW 3.17
MARK 1.11
LUKE 3.22

KEY QUOTE
And he was transfigured before them, and his clothes became dazzling white, such as no one on earth could bleach them. And there appeared to them Elijah with Moses, who were talking with Jesus.
MARK 9.2–4

30-SECOND TEXT
Tim Muldoon

At the Transfiguration, the apostles glimpse Jesus' glory—a foretaste of what is yet to come through his death, Resurrection, and Ascension.

THE BIRTH OF CHRISTIANITY

Antioch Founded in 300 BCE by Seleucis I, King of Syria, the city of Antioch stood close to the present-day Turkish city of Antakya. Many members of the early Church fled there from persecution in Jerusalem, and it was in Antioch that believers first came to be called Christians (Acts 11.26). A vibrant Christian community developed there, which later sent financial aid back to the Church in Jerusalem (Acts 11.27–30), and the apostle Paul clearly spent some time there. It should not be confused with Antioch in Pisidia, to which Paul also traveled during his missionary journeys.

canonical Accepted as Scripture; part of the accepted Jewish or Christian Bible.

Epistle A letter, especially one written for formal or teaching purposes. In the New Testament, there are twenty-one of these, mostly attributed to the apostle Paul. They were addressed to individual churches—such as Romans or Corinthians—or, in four cases, to specific individuals: Philemon, Titus, and Timothy (to whom Paul wrote twice).

heterodox Unorthdox; not conforming to established beliefs.

Holy Spirit Understood by Christians as the third Person of the Trinity (alongside God the Father and God the Son), this refers to the invisible presence and power of God at work in the world and human lives. The Hebrew term for spirit, ruach, means literally "breath of God." In the New Testament, the Holy Spirit is understood to bestow special gifts upon God's people and to inculcate in them the fruits of love, joy, peace, patience, kindness, generosity, faithfulness, gentleness, and self-control (Galatians 5.22–23).

Pentecost This is the Greek and Latin name for the Jewish feast of Shavuot, meaning "Festival of Weeks"—an annual celebration of harvest. In the Church, however, it is celebrated as the day on which the Holy Spirit fell upon the apostles, enabling them to preach the gospel to the crowds who had gathered in Jerusalem to celebrate the festival, each hearing them in their own tongue.

Sevens in the Book of Revelation

The number seven—sacred as the number of days in creation—is used fifty-five times in the book of Revelation, and the word "seventh" occurs five times. Specifically, Revelation refers to the following:

Seven angels
Seven churches (Ephesus, Smyrna, Pergamos, Thyatira, Sardis, Philadelphia, Laodicea)
Seven diadems
Seven eyes
Seven golden bowls
Seven golden lampstands
Seven heads
Seven horns
Seven kings
Seven flaming torches
Seven plagues
Seven mountains
Seven seals
Seven spirits of God
Seven stars
Seven thunders
Seven trumpets

The Seven Blessings

The following seven verses in the book of Revelation speak of special blessings reserved for God's faithful people:

1. Blessed is the one who reads aloud the words of the prophecy, and blessed are those who hear and who keep what is written in it. (Revelation 1.3)
2. Blessed are the dead who from now on die in the Lord. (Revelation 14.13)
3. Blessed is the one who stays awake and is clothed, not going about naked and exposed to shame. (Revelation 16.15)
4. Blessed are those who are invited to the marriage supper of the Lamb. (Revelation 19.9)
5. Blessed and holy are those who share in the first Resurrection. (Revelation 20.6)
6. Blessed is the one who keeps the words of the prophecy of this book. (Revelation 22.7)
7. Blessed are those who wash their robes, so that they will have the right to the tree of life and may enter the city by the gates. (Revelation 22.14)

A Sevenfold Challenge

Revelation issues the following challenge seven times (2.7; 2.11; 2.17; 2.29; 3.6; 3.13; 3.22): "Let anyone who has an ear listen to what the Spirit is saying to the churches."

RESURRECTION APPEARANCES

the 30-second bible

3-SECOND SERMON
Jesus appears to several of his followers, assuring them that although he was dead and buried, he has risen and is very much alive.

3-MINUTE MEDITATION
The post-Resurrection stories are carefully crafted to deliver a message to the earliest followers of Jesus: not only that he has conquered death, but that he still lives in flesh and blood. He eats with the disciples, shows them his wounds, and reassures them that he is not a ghost. God the Father has raised him to new life, and now Jesus sends them on a mission to preach this good news to all people.

In all four Gospels, women are the first to discover that the tomb is empty, but whereas in John Mary Magdalene is the first actually to meet with the risen Jesus—initially mistaking him, in her grief, for a gardener—in Matthew she is partnered by "the other Mary," while in Mark and Luke the women simply rush back to tell the disciples, who initially refuse to believe them. Luke records next how two of Jesus' followers are met by him on the road from Jerusalem to Emmaus, but fail to recognize him until he breaks bread with them (Mark 16.12–13 probably alludes to this encounter). In Mark, Luke, and John, Jesus suddenly stands among his disciples, despite the door to their room being locked. According to John, Thomas is absent when this happens and only accepts that Jesus has risen once he sees him for himself and touches his wounds. The four Gospels end with Jesus commissioning the disciples for service, the most detailed account (John's) detailing how he helps them to secure a great catch of fish—a metaphorical reference to their future role as preachers of the gospel— and then charges Peter to feed "his sheep," indicating the pastoral role Peter will fulfill within the early Church.

CHAPTER & VERSE
See
MATTHEW 28.1–20
MARK 16.1–20
LUKE 24.1–53
JOHN 20.1–21.25

RELATED STORIES
See also
ACTS 1.1–9, 10.40–41, 13.30–31
1 CORINTHIANS 15.3–8

KEY QUOTE
He said to them, "Why are you frightened, and why do doubts arise in your hearts? Look at my hands and my feet; see that it is I myself. Touch me and see; for a ghost does not have flesh and bones as you see that I have."
LUKE 24.36–39

30-SECOND TEXT
Tim Muldoon

Jesus alive and risen? If the empty tomb failed to convince his followers, his appearing by their side removed all doubt.

PENTECOST

the 30-second bible

3-SECOND SERMON
The Holy Spirit comes upon the apostles, allowing them to speak in new tongues and empowering them to bring the gospel to all nations.

3-MINUTE MEDITATION
Pentecost reverses the Tower of Babel, an earlier biblical episode where humanity's speech was not unified but dispersed. At Pentecost, the Holy Spirit overcomes the fracturing of humanity, as the many nations gathered are able to understand the preaching of the apostles. Only through the Holy Spirit's healing and transformative effects can such unity be restored—unity within our own selves and within the human family, both of which have been torn asunder by sin.

Before Jesus ascended into heaven, he told the apostles to wait "for the promise of the Father" (Acts 1.4), referring to the outpouring of the Holy Spirit, which occurred at Pentecost. The Holy Spirit came upon the apostles as tongues of fire (Acts 2.3), giving them the ability to speak in other languages. People from various nations were in Jerusalem at the time, and to their amazement they all understood the preaching of the apostles in their own native tongue. The apostles were then empowered to proclaim the Cross and Resurrection of Jesus Christ with boldness—remarkably given that following Jesus' arrest, they had been in hiding until they met with him again after his Resurrection; only the apostle John had remained with Christ to the end. But after the outpouring of the Holy Spirit at Pentecost, the apostles publicly proclaim Jesus as Israel's Messiah. In order to explain the meaning of these events, Peter quotes from the prophet Joel, who foretold the gift of the Spirit (Acts 2.16–18; Joel 2.28–29). For the Old Testament prophets in general, the coming of the Spirit signaled the presence of a new age—the dawning of the Messianic era. Thus, what the Israelites had long hoped and prayed for, the apostles here proclaim as coming to fruition in their very midst.

CHAPTER & VERSE
See
ACTS 2.1–42

RELATED STORIES
See also
THE TOWER OF BABEL
page 30
JEREMIAH 31.31–34
EZEKIEL 36.24–28
JOEL 2.28–29

KEY QUOTE
Peter, standing with the eleven, raised his voice and addressed them . . . "No, this is what was spoken through the prophet Joel: 'In the last days it will be, God declares, that I will pour out my Spirit upon all flesh.'"
ACTS 2.14, 16–17

30-SECOND TEXT
Andrew D. Swafford

From twelve uncertain men, fearful of the future, the apostles were transformed at Pentecost into fearless ambassadors for Christ.

THE MARTYRDOM OF STEPHEN

the 30-second bible

Stephen, one of seven men appointed to serve within the early Church, swiftly earns a reputation as a man of God due to the wonders and signs he performs. Opponents of the Church, fearing Stephen's growing influence, stir up a crowd against him, drag him to trial before the Jewish council, and set up false witnesses to testify against him. Called to account for himself, Stephen—his face reportedly like that of an angel—accuses his listeners of opposing God's Holy Spirit, likening their betrayal and murder of the promised Christ to the way that God's ministers of redemption in Israel's past, such as Joseph and Moses, repeatedly met with rejection and persecution. He further provokes his audience, many of whom were pilgrims, by defying the idea that God, creator of heaven and earth, would confine his habitation to the Temple. Enraged, his listeners drag Stephen out of the city and stone him. Before he dies, however, he echoes Jesus' words from the Cross, praying, "Lord Jesus, receive my spirit," and then, with a loud cry, "Lord, do not hold this sin against them." Stephen's martyrdom, coupled with subsequent persecution orchestrated by Saul, who stood by as Stephen was killed, led many followers of Jesus to flee Jerusalem, disseminating the gospel further afield.

3-SECOND SERMON
Stephen is stoned to death for his faith, becoming the Church's first martyr.

3-MINUTE MEDITATION
Striking parallels characterize the martyrdoms of Stephen and Jesus. Both men appear before a council, have false witnesses brought against them, announce the destruction of the Temple, and ask God to forgive their killers. Both deaths strike fear into the hearts of Jesus' followers yet lead finally to the spread of the gospel. The death of Jesus enables the Church's inauguration; that of Stephen contributes to its expansion.

CHAPTER & VERSE
See
ACTS 6.5–8.4

RELATED STORIES
See also
DEUTERONOMY 17.6–7, 18.15–19
MALACHI 1.11
MATTHEW 26.59–61
ACTS 22.17–21

KEY QUOTE
You stiff-necked people, uncircumcised in heart and ears, you are forever opposing the Holy Spirit, just as your ancestors used to do.
ACTS 7.51

30-SECOND TEXT
Stefan Bosman

Furious at Stephen's teaching, a mob stoned him to death. But although they silenced him, they could not silence his message.

THE CONVERSION OF PAUL

the 30-second bible

Having approvingly watched the stoning of Stephen, Saul of Tarsus (a town in modern-day Turkey) proceeds to ravage the early Church—going into people's homes and dragging followers of "The Way" off to prison. He secures permission from the high priest to hunt them down in the synagogue in Damascus, but on the road there he is blinded by a dazzling light from heaven and hears the voice of Jesus asking Saul why he is persecuting him. Told to go to the city and await instructions, he is visited by a disciple named Ananias, who restores his sight, having been told by Jesus in a vision that Saul is to make his name known among the gentiles. To the amazement of those he had previously persecuted, Saul—who from Acts 13.9 onward is referred to as Paul—receives the gift of the Holy Spirit, is baptized, and begins a series of missionary journeys that will occupy him for the rest of his life. So dramatic is Paul's conversion from Pharisee to Christian that he later described himself as "a Hebrew born of Hebrews; as to the Law, a Pharisee; as to zeal, a persecutor of the church; as to righteousness under the law, blameless. Yet whatever gains I had, these I have come to regard as loss because of Christ" (Philippians 3.5–7).

3-SECOND SERMON
Saul, a zealous persecutor of the Church, has his life turned around in a dramatic encounter on the Damascus road.

3-MINUTE MEDITATION
Paul is best known for his many letters to the early Christian communities throughout the Roman Empire. In several of these, he reflects on his calling as an apostle, mindful of God's mercy in light of his early desire to kill Christians: "I am the least of the apostles, unfit to be called an apostle, because I persecuted the church of God" (1 Corinthians 15.9). His conversion experience led him to emphasize the power of God's grace over obedience to the Law of Moses.

CHAPTER & VERSE
ACTS 9.3–9

RELATED STORIES
ACTS 22.3–21, 26.9–18;
1 CORINTHIANS 9.1–2, 15.3–8
GALATIANS 1.13–17
PHILIPPIANS 3.5–9

KEY QUOTE
He fell to the ground and heard a voice saying to him, "Saul, Saul, why do you persecute me?" He asked, "Who are you, Lord?" The reply came, "I am Jesus, whom you are persecuting."
ACTS 9.4–5

30-SECOND TEXT
Tim Muldoon

In, literally, one blinding moment of illumination, Paul is confronted by Christ, and from being chief persecutor of the Church he becomes its greatest ambassador.

PAUL'S LETTER TO THE ROMANS

the 30-second bible

3-SECOND SERMON

More influential than any other Epistle, the Letter to the Romans unpacks the mystery of Christian salvation and its relationship to the faith of Israel.

3-MINUTE MEDITATION

Salvation can be described as the gift of divine "sonship," a participation in Christ's relation to the Father. This familial framework should lead us to think of God more along the lines of Father than of judge—as one who deals with us in the family room rather than courtroom. While a father expects more from his children than any judge might ask for, the mercy he extends will likewise always be infinitely greater.

This most mature of St. Paul's Epistles was probably written toward the end of his third missionary journey (Acts 18.23–21.16), probably 57 or 58 CE—just a few years prior to his probable martyrdom at the hands of Emperor Nero in 62 CE. Prominently, it concerns: (1.) salvation in Christ (chs. 1–8) and (2.) the restoration of Israel (chs. 9–11)—the final chapters (ch.12–16) focus on application. First, Paul expounds the problem to which Christ is the answer: namely, sin's universal grip upon all humanity, both Jew and gentile, with no distinction. Christ's death and Resurrection have broken this bondage, inaugurating a new covenant, accessible now through faith, not "works of law" (3.28). In chapter five, Paul draws a parallel between Adam and Christ: in Adam, all die, but in Christ, all are made alive. Salvation, then, is a matter of going from being in Adam to being in Christ—and this, says Paul, occurs in baptism. The second section climaxes with Paul's declaration that "all Israel will be saved" (11.26), a phrase that likely refers to Jesus' restoration of Israel through the formation of the new covenant Church, the "Israel of God," as Paul says elsewhere (Galatians 6.16)—a "catholic" family of God that now includes both Jews and gentiles.

CHAPTER & VERSE

See
ROMANS 1.1–16.27

RELATED STORIES

See also
GENESIS 12.1–3, 15.6, 22.16–18

KEY QUOTE

For all who are led by the Spirit of God are children of God. For you did not receive a spirit of slavery to fall back into fear, but you have received a spirit of adoption. When we cry, "Abba! Father!" it is the very Spirit bearing witness with our spirit that we are children of God, and if children, then heirs, heirs of God and joint heirs with Christ—if, in fact, we suffer with him so that we may also be glorified with him.
ROMANS 8.14–17

30-SECOND TEXT

Andrew D. Swafford

Paul's letters were so valued within the Church that they later became accepted as Scripture.

PAUL

The most influential early
Christian missionary, the apostle Paul
dominates the Epistles, two-thirds of which
are ascribed to him (although the authorship
of half of these is questioned by scholars).
Paul's teaching is subtle and complex, but
centers on the idea of salvation through
faith instead of through works of the Law
(Romans 9.30–32). His ministry focuses on
the non-Jewish communities of Christians
and he develops a distinctive theology in
which Jesus' death and Resurrection establish
a new covenant (or "new testament") between
God and humanity. This leads him into
passionate debates with Peter and other
apostles over whether gentile Christians
should be bound to Jewish rituals and
practices, such as circumcision.

Paul's theology reflects his own life: most
centrally, his dramatic conversion on the road
to Damascus from zealous persecutor of
Christians to ardent follower of Christ (see
pages 144–145). Little detail beyond this
is given of his early life, other than that
he originated from Tarsus (in modern-day
Turkey) but was raised in Jerusalem by
Gamaliel, a leading figure there in the Jewish
Council known as the Sanhedrin.

Paul's conversion experience leads him
to devote the rest of his life to promoting
Christianity and writing to the nascent
Christian communities he founds. The precise
details of his travels are uncertain—he seems
to have been based in Antioch after his
conversion and to have made frequent trips
to Jerusalem—but the book of Acts describes
three missionary journeys that, between them,
take him to most of the countries bordering
the Mediterranean and involve him in
numerous local controversies.

His final journey is to Rome, where—
following various court cases before Jewish
and Roman authorities in Jerusalem after some
"Jews from Asia" accuse him of corrupting the
sanctity of the Temple by allowing non-Jews to
enter—he goes for trial, having invoked his
right as a Roman citizen to appeal to Caesar.
According to Acts, Paul is placed under house
arrest in Rome but continues to preach there.
Somewhat surprisingly, his death is not
recorded, but traditionally he is said to have
been beheaded in the reign of Nero.

Although some accuse the apostle Paul of having turned the simple
teaching of Jesus into a religion of complex doctrine, there can be
no disputing his massive contribution to the life of the Christian
Church. His amazing dynamism helped to transform a small Jewish
sect into a major world faith, taking it beyond Judea into much of
the Roman Empire. Without him, the Church's story might have
been very different.

THE BOOK OF REVELATION

the 30-second bible

3-SECOND SERMON
In dramatic fashion, Revelation unpacks the meaning of first-century events with exquisite symbolism, attempting to distill the full implications of the Cross.

3-MINUTE MEDITATION
Although Revelation is not primarily about the end of the world, its meaning can be directed thereto secondarily. In the Jewish mind, the fall of the Temple would symbolically foreshadow the end of the world, because creation was understood as a "macro-temple," and the Temple as a "microcosm" of creation. In this sense, the book's prophetic language can speak through the historical to the transcendent—through the destruction of the Temple to the end of creation.

The book of Revelation begins

with seven "letters" addressed to specific churches in Asia Minor (chs. 2–3), before turning to the worship taking place in heaven (4–5)—at the center of which is Jesus, presented as a victorious but slain lamb. From a heavenly vantage point, Revelation depicts the ushering in of the new covenant and the giving way of the Old, describing this transition through a series of "sevens": "seven seals" (6.1–8.5), "seven trumpets" (8.6–11.19), and "seven bowls" (15.7–16.21). These scenes dramatically culminate in the destruction of the "harlot city" (17–18), which then gives way to the "New Jerusalem," the heavenly bride of Christ who comes down from heaven (19, 21–22). Other memorable characters include: a "woman," a "great dragon," St. Michael the archangel, Satan, a "beast" from the sea, and "another beast" from the land, which is also called the "false prophet." The "harlot city" is usually thought to be ancient Rome or Jerusalem. Because it is also called the "great city" and the "city where their Lord was crucified" (11.8), the latter seems most likely—in which case, the book of Revelation is primarily about the destruction of the Jerusalem Temple in 70 CE.

CHAPTER & VERSE
See
REVELATION 1.1–22.21

RELATED STORIES
See also
ISAIAH 13.9–10
MATTHEW 23.29–38, 24.1–2, 15–16, 29–31, 34

3-SECOND VERSE
And I saw the holy city, the New Jerusalem, coming down out of heaven from God, prepared as a bride adorned for her husband . . . for the first things have passed away. . . . And the one who was seated on the throne said, "See, I am making all things new."
REVELATION 21.2, 4–5

30-SECOND TEXT
Andrew D. Swafford

With its elaborate structure and symbolism, Revelation has spawned all kinds of speculation, yet at heart it is simply a call to faith in adversity.

THE APOCRYPHAL GOSPELS

the 30-second bible

For many years, the existence of the apocryphal Gospels was known only through fragments quoted by early Church writers. The Gospel of the Ebionites and The Gospel of the Hebrews are examples of these "fragmentary Gospels." However, the discovery in 1945 of a collection of codices buried around 1,600 years ago in the desert in Nag Hammadi, Egypt, revealed an array of putatively apostolic recollections of Jesus' life. It is not clear to what extent the accounts reworked the material of the canonical Gospels, shared the same source material, or used independent sources. Some of the apocryphal Gospels focused on Jesus' childhood. In The Infancy Gospel of Thomas, for example, the child Jesus, Thomas' twin, performs miraculous and not entirely benevolent feats. The "Sayings Gospels," such as The Gospel of Thomas, focus on Jesus' teaching, with inclusions that clearly reflect a Gnostic influence. There are also "Resurrection Gospels" and dialogs that expand on the canonical material describing appearances of the risen Lord. While the apocryphal accounts are generally regarded as theologically dubious, they are of historical interest to New Testament scholars eager to examine the spread of early Christianity and the way in which the tradition was harmonized with other religious beliefs.

3-SECOND SERMON
Alongside the four canonical Gospels are accounts of Jesus' life and ministry that follow their form and content to some degree, while departing from them in theologically significant ways.

3-MINUTE MEDITATION
These "Gospels" bear the hallmarks of groups deemed heterodox by early Church theologians. The Nag Hammadi codices, in particular, demonstrate the influence at the time of Gnosticism: a broad spectrum of beliefs and practices which, contrary to the Christian view, claimed that salvation inheres in esoteric knowledge (gnosis) instead of in the atoning work of Christ.

CHAPTER & VERSE
See
GLOSSARY & LISTS
pages 96–97

RELATED STORIES
See also
THE APOCRYPHA
pages 92–93

KEY QUOTE
After that again he went through the village, and a child ran and dashed against his shoulder. And Jesus was provoked and said unto him: "Thou shalt not go all thy way." And immediately he fell down and died.
THE INFANCY GOSPEL OF THOMAS 4.1

30-SECOND TEXT
Liz Gulliford

The apocryphal Gospels, although not accepted as Scripture, remind us that other traditions about Jesus circulated in the early Church.

NOTES ON CONTRIBUTORS

Stefan Bosman serves as an online instructor of Biblical Hebrew at the Hebrew University of Jerusalem. He is currently a Ph.D. candidate at the University of Aberdeen and doing his research at Tyndale House in Cambridge, UK. His research focuses on Jewish exegesis in the New Testament, especially the Pauline corpus. He also contributed several articles in the field of Second Temple Judaism and Jewish-Christian relations. In another capacity, on staff at Tyndale House, he combines his two fields of training, namely as biblical scholar and software engineer.

Liz Gulliford gained her theology degree from Trinity College, Oxford, and has a Ph.D. in Theology and Religious Studies from the University of Cambridge. She has published a number of academic articles and contributed a chapter on the cinematic portrayal of Christ and the two-natures Christology to the volume *Jesus and Psychology* (Templeton Press, 2007). She co-edited *Forgiveness in Context* with Fraser Watts (T&T Clark International, 2004). Liz will shortly be taking up a Research Fellowship at the University of Birmingham.

Tim Muldoon (Ph.D., Catholic Systematic Theology, Duquesne University) is the author of five books and editor of two others on theology and spirituality, including *A Saint for All Reasons* (Langenscheidt Publishing Group, 2010). He teaches at Boston College and writes frequently for Patheos.com.

Russell Re Manning is the Lord Gifford Fellow in Natural Theology at the University of Aberdeen and Visiting Fellow of St. Edmund's College, University of Cambridge. His published works include *The Oxford Handbook of Natural Theology* (Oxford University Press, 2013), *Philosophy of Religion: The Essentials* (Hodder & Stoughton, 2012), and *30-Second Religion* (Metro Books, 2011).

Andrew D. Swafford earned his doctorate (S.T.D.) from the University of St. Mary of the Lake in Mundelein, IL, where he also earned his licentiate degree in Sacred Theology (S.T.L.). He also holds a master's degree (M.A.) in Old Testament and Semitic Languages from Trinity International University in Deerfield, IL. Currently, he is an assistant professor in the Theology department at Benedictine College in Atchison, KS, where he resides with his wife Sarah and their three children, Thomas 6, Fulton 5, and Cate 1.

RESOURCES

BOOKS

Begat: The King James Bible and the English Language
James Crystal
(Oxford University Press, 2010).

The Bible: A Very Short Introduction
John Riches
(Oxford University Press, 2000)

The Cambridge Companion to the Bible
Howard Clark Kee, Eric, M. Meyers,
John Rogerson, Amy-Jill Levine,
Anthony J. Saldarini, and Bruce Chilton
(Cambridge University Press, 2nd edn,
2007)

Catholic Bible Dictionary
Scott Hahn
(Doubleday, 2009)

The Complete Bible Handbook
John Bowker
(Dorling Kindersley, 1998)

The Eerdmans Bible Dictionary
Allen C. Myers, John W. Simpson, Philip
A. Frank, Timothy P. Jenney, and Ralph W.
Vunderink (eds)
(Eerdmans Publishing Co., 1996)

A Father Who Keeps His Promises
Scott Hahn
(Servant Books, 1998)

The Gospel of Matthew
Curtis Mitch and Edward Sri
(Baker, 2010)

The Holy Bible: New Revised Standard Version with Apocrypha
Bruce M. Metzger (ed)
(Oxford University Press, 1991)

Introducing the Old Testament
John Drane
(Fortress Press, 3rd edn, 2011)

Introducing the New Testament
John Drane
(Fortress Press, 3rd edn, 2010)

Oxford Bible Atlas
Adrian Curtis
(Oxford University Press, 4th edn, 2009)

The Oxford Bible Commentary
John Barton and John Muddiman (eds)
(Oxford University Press, 2001)

The Oxford Companion to the Bible
Bruce M. Metzger and
Michael David Coogan (eds),
(Oxford University Press, 3rd edn, 1993)

MAGAZINES/JOURNALS

Reviews in Religion and Theology
www.blackwellpublishing.com/journal.asp

Christianity Today
www.christianitytoday.com/

WEB SITES

Bible Gateway
www.biblegateway.com
A fully searchable online Bible that even lets you see different versions side by side.

Biblical Weblinks
www.biblicalweblinks.com
Maintained by scholars and librarians, this portal provides links to academically bona fide Web sites, software, books, and journals in the fields of biblical studies and Christianity.

Jewish Encyclopedia
www.jewishencyclopedia.com
This web site contains the complete twelve-volume *Jewish Encyclopedia*, which was originally published between 1901 and 1906. It provides information about Jewish life, even going back to biblical times—a great resource for the historic background of both the Old and New Testaments.

Museum of Biblical Art
www.biblicalarts.org
To see the influence of the Bible on great works of art, see the works collected at the Museum of Biblical Art.

Tyndale Toolbar
www.tyndale.cam.ac.uk/toolbar
This toolbar, compatible with most browsers, is an important aid for biblical study that can be freely accessed online, providing easy access to Bibles, translations, dictionaries, lexicons, and related literature. Hosted by Tyndale House, a residential center for biblical research in Cambridge, UK.

INDEX

ACKNOWLEDGMENTS

PICTURE CREDITS
The publisher would like to thank the following
individuals and organizations for their kind
permission to reproduce the images in this book.
Every effort has been made to acknowledge the
pictures; however, we apologize if there are any
unintentional omissions.

Akg-images/John Hios: 84.
Alamy/The Art Archive: 22.
Fotolia: 107C.
iStockphoto/ZU_09: 83B.
Library of Congress: 11B, 81B, 101B.
Shutterstock: 51BR, 153b; Zvonimir Atletic: 41C;
-BrankaVV: 126; CURAphotography: 102; Maria
Ehupova: 25TR; GoodLIfe_Studio: 70; Jurand: 129T;
Mountainpix: 148; George Muresan: 53B; Sergio
Ponomarev: 39T; Rob Rudeski: 47TR; Renata
Sedmakova: 131; Michaela Stejskalova: 29T.
Wikipedia/Romary: 119C.